I0828009

OKLAHOMA
BLACK CHEROKEES

EDITED BY
TY WILSON & KAREN COODY COOPER

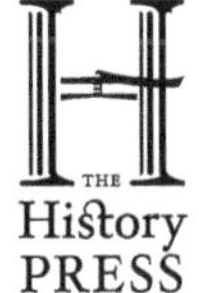

Published by The History Press
Charleston, SC
www.historypress.net

Cover: Captain Shoe Boots along with his second wife and one of their children are the subjects of an imagined painting by award-winning Cherokee artist Dan HorseChief. *Dan HorseChief.*

First published 2017

ISBN 9781540225726

Library of Congress Control Number: 2017938350

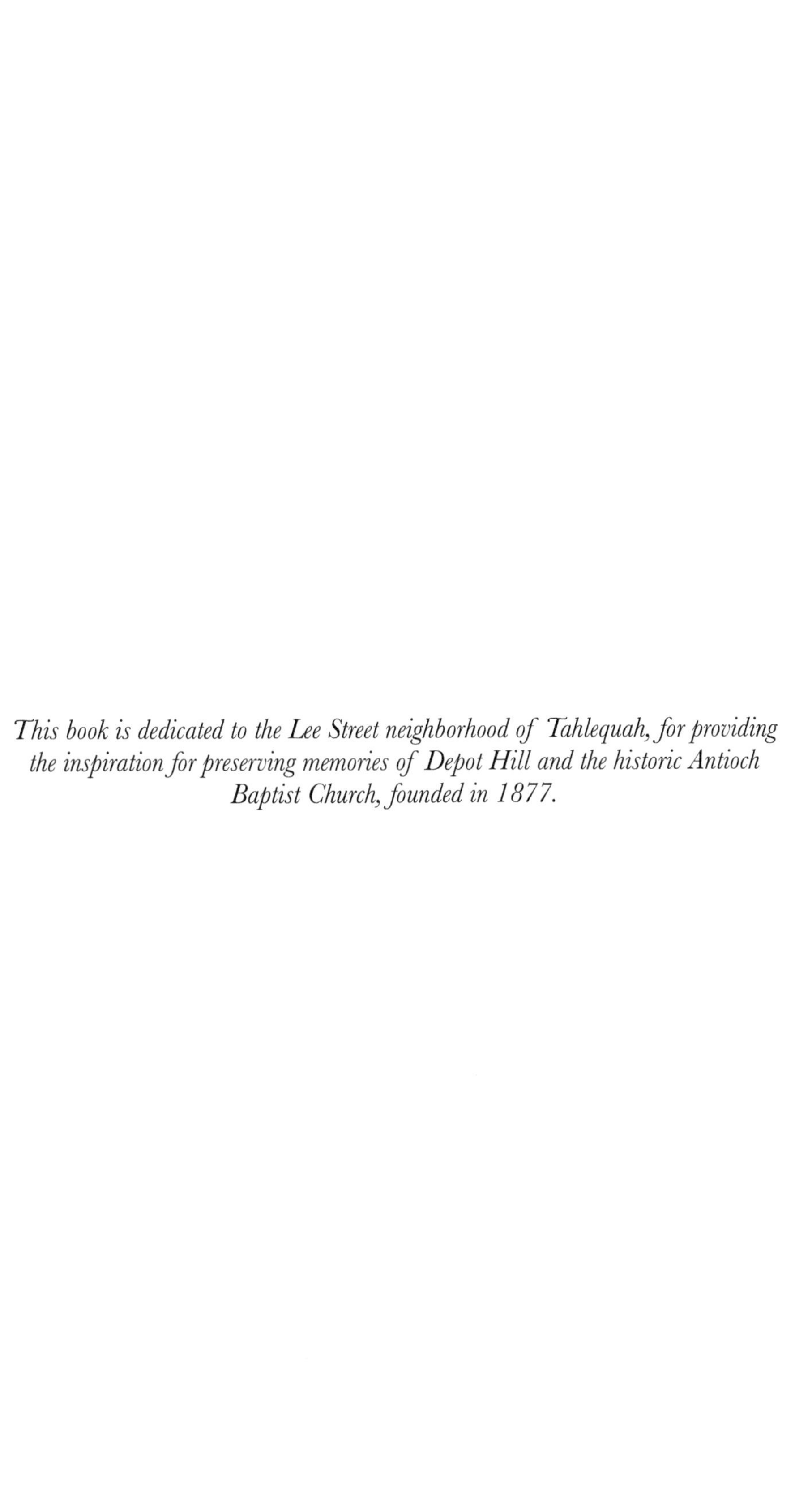

This book is dedicated to the Lee Street neighborhood of Tahlequah, for providing the inspiration for preserving memories of Depot Hill and the historic Antioch Baptist Church, founded in 1877.

CONTENTS

Contents

ACKNOWLEDGEMENTS

A special thank-you to Dan HorseChief for graciously sharing his prize-winning artwork of *Captain Shoe Boots*. Thank you to all the contributing writers, artists and photographers, as well as to the staff people of various archives and agencies who generously provided images for this project.

Cherokees for Black Indian History Preservation Foundation was organized in 2014 and undertook this book project in 2016. The support of the CBIHPF board and membership made this project possible. Current officers of the board are Joe Wilson, president; Ty Wilson, vice-president; Anita Christie, treasurer; and Antwaun Todd, secretary.

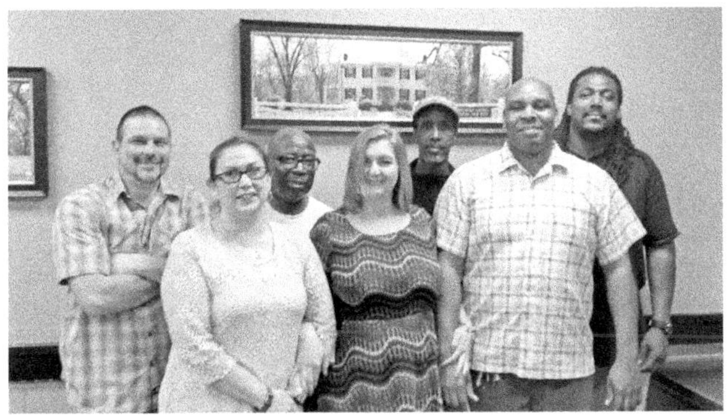

The board of the Cherokees for Black Indian History Preservation Foundation works to collect and promote inclusive history. *Aron Dunlap.*

INTRODUCTION

ONE PEOPLE, PROUD CHEROKEE

Ty Wilson, co-founder of the nonprofit Cherokees for Black Indian History Preservation Foundation (CBIHP), prefers the term *black* rather than *African American* because "Africa is far removed from my experience, and Cherokee Freedman doesn't apply because no one living today experienced slavery." This book, too, focuses on aspects of the past unfamiliar to most. A complex historical foundation is provided in this introduction so the people's lives you are about to experience can knowingly be observed.

As early centuries evolved, Cherokee citizens became a conglomerate people spread over a territory encompassing parts of five southern states. Nearly five hundred years ago, Hernando de Soto's Spanish explorers captured southeastern American Indian women (some of whom may have been Cherokee). It was recorded that a Spanish black slave aided a native woman's escape, and the two ran off together. Genetic mixing with arriving people began long ago in the Americas. Being a matrilineal society, Cherokees had always been born into the clan of the mother. Being sired by an outsider did not affect a child's destiny or acceptance into Cherokee society. For example, Chief John Ross was born to an unbroken line of Cherokee women, and despite also having had three successive male antecedents from the British Isles, Ross was entirely Cherokee by Cherokee standards. However, white antagonists accused him of being a white man posing as an Indian.

A century after De Soto's visit, colonization of the Americas began in earnest. Young European-born men ventured into Appalachia, while Hispanic colonies operated in Florida and French trappers hunted and traded on the Great Plains and inhabited New Orleans. Cherokee absorption of Shawnee refugees in the seventeenth century reflected a practice occurring throughout the ages of Cherokee existence. Soon, white husbands of Cherokee women adopted southern plantation life. Black slaves became common in Cherokee enterprises. Cherokee matrilineal clan organization was soon abandoned.

Many accommodations were made with the hope of gaining acceptance from the ever-encroaching population of white Americans, yet the Cherokee population was eventually forced to move outside the existing United States. Traversing the Trail of Tears were full-blood, white-mixed and black-mixed Cherokees, along with adopted whites, black slaves, remnant Natchez and Euchee Indians and white missionaries, all arriving in the West to build new plantations, subsistence farms, missions and businesses.

The 1851 census of the Cherokee Nation in Indian Territory revealed a total population nearing 18,000. That population included 1,844 slaves and 64 free blacks. Internal Cherokee political groupings over time have included Upper, Lower and Middle Towns; Chickamauga insurgents; Old Settlers; Treaty Party; Full-bloods (about cultural attributes rather than bloodline); Keetoowah; black Cherokees; white Cherokees and so on. Today, the population of the Cherokee Nation, as a political entity, has less to do with race, color or cultural practice than with a single roll prepared prior to Oklahoma statehood from which many black Cherokee by blood applicants were deflected. While the numbers of erroneously filed individuals may seem inconsequential, the practice of targeting black Cherokee by blood applicants was willful and injurious.

With Oklahoma statehood in 1907, Cherokee Nation government was shut down. Dawes enrollees received allotments of Cherokee land, divided among 8,703 full-bloods, 27,916 mixed bloods, 286 adopted whites and 4,919 Freedmen for a total of 41,824 allotments amounting to 4,346,145 acres, according to historian Angie Debo in *And Still the Waters Run*.

Extensive Dawes Commission interviews recorded parents, marriages, siblings and slave owners, with the information surviving as a precious gift to historians and family genealogists. Two major Cherokee rolls taken in preparation of allotting land before statehood includes the "Cherokee by blood" roll and "Freedmen" roll (for former Cherokee slaves and their descendant residents). Cherokee by blood listings should have included any resident black Cherokees who had proof or responsible testaments of Cherokee-blood antecedents; however, enumerators excluded many eligible black Cherokee citizens by summarily listing them on the Freedmen roll (including a line of proven descendants of the esteemed Chief John Ross family—see the Allen Lynch story).

The lists were not expected to have a future use beyond allotment prior to statehood, so at the time, few people being mislabeled protested formally. Dawes commissioners were often overbearing and demeaning when interviewing black applicants. Protests came mostly from those applicants who were removed entirely or were barred from being listed at all. However, when the Cherokee Nation reconstituted in the mid-twentieth century, Cherokee leadership selected only the Cherokee by blood roll to serve as the basis for future citizenship. David Cornsilk, during his term as a Cherokee tribal enrollment employee in the 1980s, noted that one-third of the Dawes Freedman applications had referenced Native ancestry. Federal policy, however, allows tribes to determine their own citizenship requirements, and courts resist interfering.

Race is scientifically nonexistent because no single definition of race stands up to scrutiny, yet race is constantly an issue in today's world. Color of skin often erroneously serves as a stand-in for "race." While American Indians protest stereotypes of "Redskin" or "Red Man," there are still memories of a location in Tahlequah being called Nigger Hill, as noted in a study by geologist Lauret Savoy in 2015. Humans, too, often concentrate on dividing people and demeaning "Others" and spend too little effort appreciating what connects all of us.

This book focuses on black Cherokee histories, starting in the southeastern homeland, moving to Indian Territory and culminating within the fourteen counties of the Cherokee Nation in Oklahoma. The history presented here is yours; it is American history. Readers will recognize shared aspirations regarding survival, hopes and fears, losses and successes, and will be led to applaud ingenuity and courage. Let the voices speak to your heart because this history is your history. We are one people: proud Cherokee.

KAREN COODY COOPER

BLACK/CHEROKEE TIMELINE

1526	Black slaves of a Spanish colony on the Pedee River escape to live with Indians.
1540	One of Hernando de Soto's slaves helps a captive Indian chieftess escape; they marry.
1674	The Stono War prompts South Carolina to enslave tribal enemies; Cherokee warriors bring 160 Indian captives to sell in slave marketplace.
1693	Cherokee leaders complain about other tribes capturing and selling Cherokee captives (as they themselves had been doing to other tribes).
1708	Census report notes that South Carolina colonists own 2,900 African slaves along with 1,400 American Indian slaves.
1715	Black militiamen are used in colonial invasion of Cherokees, then stay to assist Cherokees in attacking Creek Indians; colonies forbid taking slaves into Cherokee Nation.
1755	Nancy Ward, Cherokee Beloved Woman, acquires first Negro slave in Cherokee Nation, given to her as the spoils of war for her bravery under fire.
1760	North Carolina passes act giving colonists the right to enslave Cherokee captives to sell at local slave markets and the West Indies.
1763	Colonies offer Cherokee people rewards for returning runaway black slaves to discourage Cherokees from adopting or raiding and freeing slaves.

1775	"Nothing can be more alarming to the Carolinas than the idea of an attack from Indians and Negroes," reports a colonist. Divide-and-conquer stance is adopted.
1820	The Cherokee Council forbids slaves purchasing liquor and forbids Cherokees purchasing goods from slaves. Each village is advised to patrol and enforce fines.
1827	Cherokee government, largely managed by slaveholders, establishes laws excluding blacks from participating in Cherokee government.
1835	About 17 percent of Cherokee Nation has white ancestry, and 78 percent of families owning slaves have white blood, according to Theda Perdue's *Slavery and the Evolution of Cherokee Society*.
1838–39	Cherokees and their slaves suffer the Trail of Tears. Lewis Ross quickly imports five hundred more slaves needed for building the new Cherokee Nation.
1840	Cherokee Nation makes it illegal for any free Negro or mulatto not of Cherokee blood to own improvements, and sheriffs are empowered to confiscate said items.
1841	Cherokee Nation law instructs patrols to pick up blacks who lack a pass and punish any found with a weapon; also, all are forbidden from teaching writing and reading to free blacks or slaves.
1842	Serious Cherokee slave riot occurs. New law directs free blacks not freed by Cherokees to leave the Nation; owners freeing slaves are made responsible for their conduct.
1846	A plot planning a second slave riot is squelched by slave owner Lewis Ross.
1848	New law states that any white person providing instruction to blacks would be expelled. Despite repressive laws, many Cherokees choose to ignore the laws.
1851–52	Free black family of Abraham Moore leaves the Cherokee Nation for Liberia; escaped Cherokee slave Henry Bibb becomes a published abolitionist in Canada.
1861	John Ross seeks Civil War neutrality; Stand Watie leads Confederate faction; violence causes many to flee to Kansas or Texas; Chief goes to Pennsylvania/Washington, D.C.; slaves become soldiers.

1866	Postwar agreements between Cherokee Nation and the United States call for Cherokee Freedmen entitlement use of Cherokee land and citizen rights.
1875–95	Six Freedmen are elected to, and serve on, the Cherokee National Council over a twenty-year period.
1877	Antioch Baptist Church is founded in Tahlequah. The area later becomes known as Depot Hill when train service is provided.
1898	Curtis Act shutters tribal government. The Dawes Commission creates rolls for final land allotments. Cherokee Nation buildings and properties are disbursed to state possession.
1907	Oklahoma becomes the forty-sixth state in a ceremony portraying a cowboy marrying an American Indian woman.
1937	Indian-Pioneer Papers, a Works Progress Administration project, undertakes interviews of a sampling of Oklahoma citizens, including Cherokees and Freedmen.
1941	Jesse Bartley Milam receives presidential appointment as Cherokee Nation chief during land-use negotiations with GRDA, and he begins developing Cherokee projects.
1963	Cherokee National Historical Society opens a museum with a plaster cast statue of Charlene White representing a black Cherokee woman on the Trail of Tears.
1971	General elections restored to Cherokee Nation by President Reagan; voter cards are distributed to Freedmen and Cherokees; W.W. Keeler is elected chief.
1983	Chief Ross Swimmer decrees that Cherokee Certificate of Degree of Indian Blood (CDIB) is required for voting; Freedmen seek to regain citizenship status.
1997	Antioch Church in Tahlequah is firebombed and then restored.
2013	Former slave cemetery in Park Hill is located by use of ground-penetrating radar (the lost cemetery had been mentioned in 1937 interviews).
2015	Cherokees for Black Indian History Preservation Foundation (CBIHP) becomes a 501(c)3 nonprofit service group aligned with the Cherokee Nation Community Cultural Outreach program.

CHAPTER 1

SEVEN CHEROKEE NATION FAMILIES

Karen Coody Cooper

The following brief histories follow Cherokees caught up in the quickly changing legal landscape of Cherokee citizenship. The Cherokee tribe became a progressive people living in northwest Georgia, northeast Alabama, Tennessee and the western portions of the Carolinas. Regrettably, Cherokee leaders chose to adopt institutionalized slavery (the first black slave was gifted to Cherokee Beloved Woman, Nancy Ward, in 1755). The majority of Cherokee citizens did not acquire black slaves (early Cherokees, however, had employed temporary enslavement of captives). As white frontiersmen increasingly married Cherokee women, plantation life was embraced as a means of economic development, and black slave numbers grew. Probably the first black slaves working on the land of what is now the Cherokee Nation in Oklahoma were those of Jean Pierre Chouteau, French trader involved with the Osage Indians at his trading post, ferry and saline works at Salina, established in 1796. One of Chouteau's slaves at his home in St. Louis, Marguerite Scypion, set a precedent by suing for her freedom in 1805 and winning her case in 1838. Freedom was to come much later for most enslaved people. The following brief accounts focus on the lives of people caught up in the tragedy of human bondage in the Cherokee Nation.

In about 1800, Bob, a slave owned by Archibald Coody, produced a Cherokee son with a Cherokee woman (identity unknown). The resulting child grew up as a Cherokee citizen known as James Coody. Since James was born to a Cherokee woman, he was Cherokee by rule of matrilineal descent (in practice at the time) and born to freedom in the Cherokee Nation even though his father remained a slave. Dark-skinned James Coody grew up to marry a white woman. Regarding the marriage of Coody to Polly Cart(er), James had to post bond of $1,250 in case someone were to prove they were not marrying within the law of the time (Roane County Tennessee files of December 29, 1819). William McKarney stated in a deposition that he performed the marriage of the couple in the fall of 1819.

On November 11, 1824, the Cherokee National Committee declared that "intermarriages between negro slaves and Indians, or white, shall not be lawful." Cherokee lawmakers abandoned matrilineal clan birth traditions and passed a law restricting with whom Cherokee women should procreate. The law was not retroactive, and James retained his Cherokee citizen status.

James Coody opted to join the Cherokees who had moved west and relocated his family to "Arkansaw," accepting lands there. He initiated several efforts to receive compensation for the improvements he left behind, and those accountings have provided most of the information that we know about James. We find he had a son, Robert, resident of Skin Bayou, Cherokee Nation, named in testimony before the judge of the Cherokee Nation in April 1845 as his only living child.

James was well represented in his long, drawn-out case seeking restitution for the property from which he had been driven. Respected Cherokee citizens fully supported him as being Cherokee. William Potter Ross, John Drew, Stephen Foreman, Looney Riley, Caleb Starr, Wiley Tuten (married to Cherokee citizen Rachel Coodey) and others sent letters of support, provided depositions and represented his case. It seems white authorities in Tennessee chose to turn their backs on James in favor of local white cronies who were then living on his land and enjoying the buildings and fences he had left behind.

His son, Robert Coody, is found on the 1880 Cherokee census with a wife named Martha, listed as white, living in Illinois district. It is not known when Robert died, but Martha lived to make an application, at the age of sixty-two, for Dawes enrollment as a white woman having been married to a Cherokee, but she died before September 1, 1902. Nothing further is known of Robert.

In another story, Robert C. Smith reported that his grandmother, a Cherokee woman, decided that her slave, Smith's grandfather, would make a good husband. Tragically, when the grandmother later died in Indian Territory, Smith's grandfather, as well as the couple's daughter and their son, Dave (both half Cherokee), were sold to Chief John Ross, and then Dave was traded to an owner named Tibbetts in Arkansas. Having never before been treated as a slave, the young and burly Dave was given a whipping by his new owner, and Dave was subsequently jailed in Fayetteville for fighting back. Dave was to be held in a cell until someone purchased him. During an attempted breakout by a pair of incarcerated criminals, Dave saved the life of the jailor, Presley R. Smith, who promptly purchased Dave and treated him like a free man again. Dave married a woman owned by Smith, and the couple adopted the Smith surname and raised a family who became free at the Civil War's end. Their children (including Robert C. Smith) never were recognized as Cherokee by blood.

Freedman Henry Henderson's father was said to be Cherokee citizen Martin Vann. Henry and Martin, however, never had a father-son relationship because Henry was born in 1843 into the status of slave. Henry and his mother, Katie Vann, were owned by a member of the Vann family of the Cherokee Nation, and Katie had been loaned to Martin Vann. Katie Vann reported in Dawes interviews of 1901 that she named her son in memory of a lover she'd once had. That was the sweetest revenge she could take.

Henry never had the opportunity to be listed as Cherokee by blood, even though one parent was Cherokee. The best he could hope for was to be accepted as a Freedman. In a Works Progress Administration (WPA) interview, he enumerated his ensuing successes as a Freedman farmer of extensive lands and as a carter managing three oxen teams. Being a Cherokee Freedman provided advantages above other freed southern slaves, but for someone raised as Henry was, speaking Cherokee language and having a Cherokee father, being enrolled as a Freedman fell short of justice.

The practice of using *B* for black and *M* for mulatto when listing slaves on inventory lists and census records allows one to see evidence of a slave owner or overseer having fathered children of a dark-skinned slave mother where she is noted by the letter *B* and her children are noted *M*. There was a time when slave-owning men justified their act of inseminating slave women by asserting that they intended to improve the product. That was a presumptuous and self-serving notion, and given that most owners never labored and lived under the conditions of a slave, there was no credible rationale for the practice. Further, the philandering men certainly did not improve their relationships with their Cherokee wives, daughters, mothers and sisters, all of whom generally were aware of the practice.

According to Sarah Wilson of Fort Gibson, "When I was eight years old, old Mistress died, and Grandmammy told me why old Mistress picked on me so. She told me about me being half Mister Ned's blood. Then I knowed why Mister Ned would say, 'Let her alone, she got big blood in her,' and then he would laugh."

Women on both sides of the philandering quotient resented the sexual liberties men took with slave women. Master Ned/Edward Johnson was half Cherokee. Slave Sarah was the child of her owner and his slave. She was considered a Freedman, although she was one-fourth Cherokee.

Interviews and published accounts cannot summarily be accepted as fact. For example, Milton Starr claimed to be half Cherokee in his WPA interview, saying that he had been the property of a kindly slave owner father named Jerry Starr, who Milton said was Cherokee and treated Milton as an indulged son. However, Milton's father's application for Freedman status finds that Jerry had, in fact, been the slave of George Starr, and the 1910 census noted him as black. An interview with Milton's brother, William Lee Starr, provided corrections of Milton's statements, yet it has been Milton's account that has captured the interest of researchers and writers who fail to fact-check first-person accounts. Milton had been born in about 1860 and would have had little detailed memory of living as a slave. It is possible that Jerry, the father, told son Milton that there was a claim to Cherokee blood, and he could have playfully told Milton he "owned" him, causing Milton's information to be flawed by childhood confusion. However, Milton had a knack for turning the limelight his way, as seen in a few news pieces published during his life. His fabricated life story actually led to long-term attention paid to Milton since his erroneous account is highlighted in numerous dissertations and books and is freely accessed through online websites without a caveat.

Joseph Turkey Vann, once a slave of Avery Vann, served as a soldier in the Indian Home Guards, Third Regiment, Company M, protecting Cherokee buildings and leaders during the Civil War. He had been freed in 1862 by Avery's daughter, Catherine (Katy) Williams, who inherited slaves from her father's estate. In a letter of 1903 regarding enrollment, a sentence noted of Turk's offspring, "[T]heir father was Cherokee." They were enrolled as Freedmen. Turk's wife, Clora (Chlora/Chorley), born in 1849 and living until 1924, applied and received a widow's military pension after Turk's death in the 1890s. She worked as a matron and laundress at the Cherokee Colored High School.

Son Avery gained an education and taught at the high school from 1900 to 1907. His proudest achievement, however, was becoming a voter in his teens: "I cast my first vote for chief of this Nation in August 1895, but the first vote that I cast was cast at the election of the Mayor of Tahlequah in the spring of 1895."

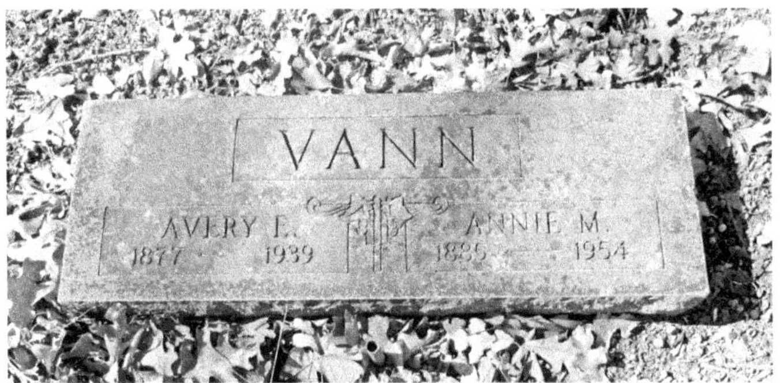

Avery Vann taught at the Cherokee Colored High School from 1900 to 1907 and was buried in Stick Ross Cemetery, Bliss Avenue, Tahlequah, in 1939. *Jim Roaix.*

Clora's granddaughter, Lelia Swepston Ross, graduated from the Cherokee Colored High School in 1908. Generations of this family are buried at Ross Cemetery on Bliss Avenue in Tahlequah. The industrious family valued education, duty, achievement, hard work and sacrifice, exemplifying the finest qualities of citizenry.

White Cherokees exist because of miscegenation; the same holds true for black Cherokee individuals. White blood, however, has often been more acceptable to Cherokee authorities than black blood. In 1871, the Cherokee court deemed that it was "authorized to decide against all cases before it wherein colored or black men are claiming citizenship from marrying black female citizens under the law 'Regulating Intermarriage with White Men,' as they are convinced a correct interpretation of said law will not authorize a clerk of any of the courts to issue a license to a black man to marry a black as it only alludes to, and was intended for white men and Cherokee women."

When Oklahoma statehood was looming, Lewis Taylor undertook the business of enrolling his Cherokee wife, Eva Rider Taylor, along with their children (Rider, Mary, Shadeck and Betsy) as Cherokee citizens by blood, while he himself enrolled as a Cherokee Freedman. The Taylor children provide an example of black Cherokees being appropriately enrolled as citizens by blood. As you read further stories, you will see that enrollment did not always occur as it should have.

History is something we share, sometimes in ways not documentable or known. Things that happened affect what is to happen. The past is prologue.

References

Ancestry.com, Fold Three and Find-a-Grave access, including Dawes enrollment papers, census and roll records, cemetery lists and so on.

Baker, T. Lindsay, and Julie P. Baker. *The WPA Oklahoma Slave Narratives.* Norman: University of Oklahoma Press, 1996. Includes the interviews of Henderson and Wilson and the inaccurate narrative of Milton Starr.

Chase, Marybelle W. *Indian Home Guards Civil War Service Records*. N.p., 1993.

Civil War pension records. Clora Vann application. Viewed at african-nativeamerican.blogspot.com, 2016.

Coody, Waymon O. Loose-leaf binder of unpublished Coody family history. A chapter on James Coody includes transcribed records from Edgefield County, South Carolina; Roane County, Tennessee; Knoxville, Tennessee; Cass County, Georgia; Hamilton County, Tennessee; and Cherokee Nation. The Roane County, Tennessee loose papers on James Coody were available online in 2016 at www.roanetnheritage.com/research/native/02.htm.

Hampton, David Keith. *Cherokee Mixed-Bloods.* Lincoln, AR: ARC Press of Cane Hill, 2005.

Indian-Pioneer Papers. Interview of William Lee Starr. University of Oklahoma, Norman, Oklahoma, 1937. Accessed 2016. https://digital.libraries.ou.edu/whc/pioneer/papers/7282%20starr.pdf.

Sturm, Circe. *Blood Politics: Race, Culture, and Identity in the Cherokee Nation of Oklahoma.* Berkeley: University of California Press, 2002.

CHAPTER 2

TEARS ON THE TRAIL

Karen Coody Cooper

The Trail of Tears became an epic touchstone for Cherokee people. The unnecessary eviction and resultant suffering of American Indian groups that had become educated and economically productive resulted from racial bias fueled by greed. Andrew Jackson gained political fame at the Battle of Horseshoe Bend, where Cherokee warriors turned the tide of the battle, making Jackson appear heroic. After Jackson became president, Cherokee land was needed to reward his cronies, and Jackson overruled a Supreme Court decision when he evicted the Cherokees. The travails of the Trail of Tears have become a symbol of survival under duress that testifies to Cherokee character, strength and endurance. Little, however, has been noted of the toils of Cherokee slaves before and during Removal and their role in rebuilding and reestablishing the Cherokee Nation's wealth at the end of the Trail.

Not all blacks trekking west with the Cherokees had been Cherokee slaves. Some migrating black individuals were Cherokee citizens by blood, and some were freed blacks who had become culturally aligned with the Cherokees, while others joined the march along the way. Cherokee John Armstrong related a story told to him by an elder Cherokee named Soskee (Soski), who recalled a black couple named John and Betsy Reece who had escaped their white owners and traveled with the Cherokees during Removal.

In April 1832, a private organizer expecting to transport 1,000 Cherokees to the West obtained only 380 subscribers (with 108 of them noted as

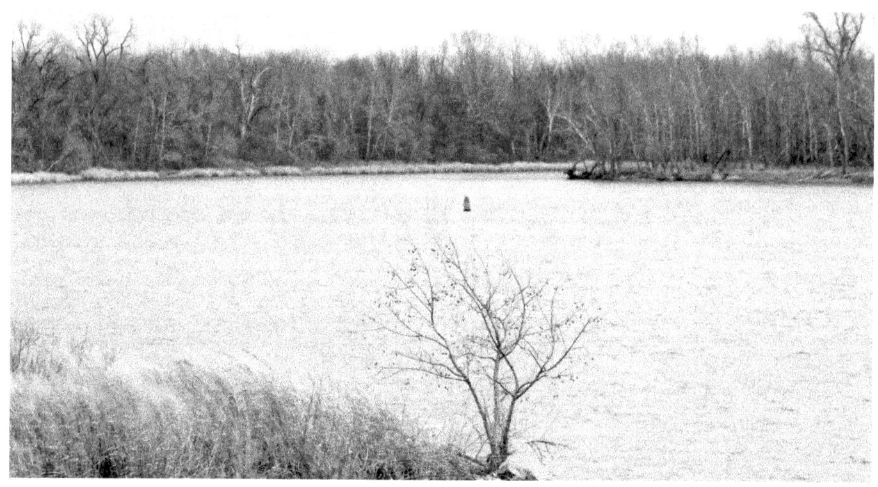

The Illinois River enters the Arkansas River from the north, where the landscape has changed very little from when Cherokee citizens first arrived in the area. *Jim Roaix.*

being black). The group was loaded onto nine flatboats to run the rapids of Muscle Shoals and then transferred to a steamboat for the remainder of the journey. While some disembarked near Fort Smith, the rest continued to the mouth of the Illinois River, where, twenty days after they had left Tennessee, they were put ashore in their new homeland without food. The destitute group ultimately received some rations from the Cherokee Indian agent, but the agent had no authority to provide food to their slaves, nor to intermarried whites.

Pickens Willis, head of a Cherokee family, left the state of Georgia in a wagon train in 1833. Grandson Nathaniel Dow Willis reported in a 1937 interview, "My grandparents were helped, and protected by some very faithful negro slaves who came out here with them. The negro slaves went ahead of the wagons with axes and guns to cut out the way for the on-coming train of wagons and to kill any wild beast they might see. The wolves were very dangerous at night, coming quite near to the campers."

Joseph Coodey and his Cherokee wife, Jane Ross Coodey, also moved west at that time. Records state that they took thirteen slaves with them: six men and seven women, all of unknown ages. However, the report at the end of the journey (with the Coodey family having lost their eldest and youngest daughters to death during the trip) cites that they arrived with only nine slaves (five men and four women), representing a loss of four people. While it is possible that a slave couple slipped away to freedom with children in tow (as did occur in some cases), it is also likely that some or all of the missing Coodey slaves suffered death on the distressing journey.

Russell Thornton's population study of the 1835 census revealed that the Tennessee Cherokee population was 56.8 percent full-blood, 21 percent half blood and 14.5 percent quarter blood, while intermarried whites were 2.9 percent of the population and mixed free Negro residents accounted for 1.2 percent of the Tennessee Cherokee population. The total number of Cherokee slaves in Tennessee, North Carolina, Georgia and Alabama was 1,592 slaves. Thornton reported that 7.4 percent of tribal members held slaves, which conversely means that more than 90 percent of the Cherokees remaining in the East in 1835 did not have slaves.

Eventually, soldiers were sent to round up the remaining Cherokees and impound them. Many died in the compounds as diseases spread from overcrowding, lack of sanitary facilities and unsafe water. The survivors in the camps were weakened from sickness and poor nutrition. The army then undertook transporting the population by groups of approximately one thousand, but soon Chief John Ross gained the right to organize the move of the remaining contingents. Even though Cherokee management of the move improved circumstances, inclement weather and delivery of quality provisions proved troublesome. Trailways were in poor condition, crossing occasional streams was hazardous, materials wore out and supplies were often poorly provisioned.

According to historian Theda Perdue, one of the seventeen groups to be removed, managed by George Hicks in 1838, included thirteen slaves among four families: Thomas Woodward had four, Te-Kah-se-na-ky had one, Philip Inlow had five and Hicks held four. Those slaves performed services benefiting the entire contingent, including setting up camp, pushing stuck wagons, serving as night watchmen and hunting game.

Author Tiya Miles reported a reference to a slave woman by name: "[K]ind Nancy [would] wash and {dry} our clothes in the evening by the fire." Slaves served their owners as teamsters, cooks, nurses, firewood gatherers and laundresses and watched over the safety of the owners' children and possessions. Accompanying slaves were generally shortchanged on sleep and personal comfort. Shoes disintegrated along the way, and Lewis Ross, in charge of supplies, was forced to purchase large orders of footwear at his own expense, seeking reimbursement at a later date.

Another tale, provided by Milton Starr during an Indian-Pioneer interview, relates that his mother had been a slave girl, Jane Coursey, whom the Cherokee Starr family confiscated when they left on the Removal march. "My mother wasn't bought, but was stole by the Indians, and when she was freed she went back to Tennessee," Starr noted.

Reading about the family of Shoe Boots, a revered Cherokee military leader, we learn that some of his adult black Cherokee children walked the Trail, while his widow and mother of his children, in company of one of their sons, traveled west via steamboat. The mode of conveyance depended on the wealth and station of individuals (or of their owners). Travel by water was faster but more expensive. Some Cherokee slave owners found it useful to purchase their own steamboats to ferry their slaves to the West as a way to more easily prevent their slaves from escaping during the journey, as well as to retain slave stamina for the work ahead.

"There were looks of astonishment and shouts of surprise as boat after boat came into view, some towing barges filled with men, women and children. As the boats drew near the shore the onlookers saw the barges were filled with black people, too many to count," historian Marguerite McFadden noted about the arrival of Joseph Vann's slaves.

Henry Henderson further reported, "Vann brought many slaves with him on a steamboat and…had his slaves clear up land and make fence rails until he had several hundred acres under cultivation in corn and cotton. He also owned about three thousand sheep which he turned loose in the hills, and he had hundreds of hogs and cattle out on the range."

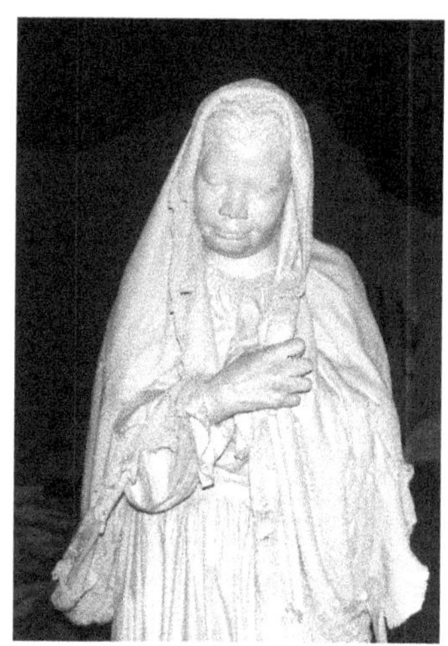

Charlene White served as the model for the Cherokee slave shown here at the 2001 opening of the Trail of Tears Exhibit at the Cherokee Heritage Center. *Jim Roaix.*

At the end of the Trail, the labor of slaves created wealth in the form of substantial government buildings, roadways, gristmills, cotton gins, bridges, ferries, chimneys, cabins, barns, springhouses and toolmaking. Slavery was the engine that drove plantation life. Slaves created Cherokee wealth by building the mansions, clearing the land, constructing fences, cultivating extensive crops, operating cotton gins and mills and managing large numbers of livestock. As they produced families, the bodies of their children added to the wealth of their owners.

Non-slaveholding Cherokees and freed blacks were left to perform their own toil, tired though they may have been from the arduous journey, often arriving just in time to be pressed to get crops planted into soil that had never before been tilled.

Currently, the Cherokee Nation and the Oklahoma Trail of Tears Association honors the graves of those who walked the Trail of Tears by placing plaques at their burial sites. Since slave graves were generally unmarked, there will be few, or no, memorials for them.

References

Baker, Jack D. *Cherokee Emigration Rolls, 1817–1835*. N.p.: Baker Publishing Company, circa 1977.

Foreman, Grant. *Indian Removal.* Norman: University of Oklahoma Press, 1932.

Miles, Tiya. *Ties that Bind.* Berkeley: University of California Press, 2005.

Mooney, James. *Myths of the Cherokee*. Reprint, Nashville, TN, 1982.

Thornton, Russell. *The Cherokees: A Population History.* Lincoln: University of Nebraska Press, 1990.

Tyner, J.W. Interview of John Armstrong, Cherokee, recorded on July 7, 1968. Western History Collections, University of Oklahoma Libraries, Norman, Oklahoma.

CHAPTER 3

FREE BLACKS IN INDIAN TERRITORY

Daniel F. Littlefield Jr. and Mary Ann Littlefield

Excerpted with the permission of Daniel F. Littlefield Jr. from "The Beams Family: Free Blacks in Indian Territory," published in Journal of Negro History *(January 1976): 17–35.*

By the time removal was completed, the number of free blacks among the Five Tribes was surprisingly large. Their population among the individual tribes varied according to the degree to which they were tolerated by the Indians. That toleration loosely corresponded to the severity of the slave codes of the tribes. The difficulty in making generalizations about the Indians' attitudes towards blacks has been pointed out in an article by William G. McLoughlin. Historians have come to contradictory conclusions, he says, because there is insufficient evidence.[1] McLoughlin demonstrates in that article and elsewhere, however, that as time passed and the Indians were drawn into the national debate over slavery, principally through their agents and missionaries, slave codes among some of the tribes became more severe.[2] Those slave codes, in most cases, had direct bearing on the attitudes towards free blacks.

There were fewer free blacks among the Cherokees, despite the large number of slaves among them. In 1835, on the eve of removal, there were 16,543 Cherokees and 1,592 slaves. By 1859, the number of slaves in the Cherokee Nation had reached 4,000. Historians agree that slavery among the Cherokees was little different from that in the white South and that the status of slaves and free blacks declined as laws became more severe.[3] After removal, the Cherokees wrote a constitution in 1839 in which they admitted to citizenship descendants of Cherokee women and black men but excluded the descendants of Cherokee men and black women. However, all persons of "negro or mulatto parentage" were excluded from holding public office. A few days after adoption of the constitution, the Cherokee Council passed a law prohibiting free citizens from marrying "any slave or person of color" who was not a citizen. Punishment could not exceed fifty lashes. A convicted black male, however, received one hundred. A law of 1840 prohibited free blacks, not of Cherokee blood, and slaves from holding improvements and other property in the nation. Such property then held by blacks was ordered sold to the highest bidder. The same law forbade free blacks to sell spirituous liquors in the nation. An 1841 law created "patrol companies" to capture and punish any slaves caught off their masters' premises without a pass and to give up to thirty-nine lashes to any black not entitled to Cherokee privileges and found carrying a weapon of any kind. The same council passed a law prohibiting the teaching of slaves and free blacks not of Cherokee blood to read or write. In the aftermath of a slave revolt, the council of 1842 passed an act which ordered all free blacks, not freed by Cherokee citizens, to leave the nation by January 1, 1843. Any who refused to leave were to be reported to the agent for expulsion. The same act provided that if a Cherokee citizen freed his slaves, he was responsible for their conduct as free blacks. If he died or left the nation, the free blacks were to give "satisfactory security" to one of the circuit judges for their conduct. The act also stated that any free black found guilty of "aiding, abetting, or decoying" slaves to leave their owners was to receive one hundred lashes. An 1848 law prohibited the teaching of *any* black to read or write. An 1855 law prohibited the hiring of teachers with abolitionist sentiments, and finally in 1859, the Council passed an act requiring all free blacks to leave the nation. This bill, however, was vetoed by Chief John Ross.[4] The free blacks in the Indian Territory attracted slave traders and hunters from many of the Southern states, particularly Arkansas, and the Republic of Texas. Slave owners filed claims for title to many of them. Some, no doubt, had valid claims to the fugitive slaves who took refuge in the enclaves of free blacks. But most were speculators who saw the somewhat anomalous condition of the free blacks as an opportunity to make huge profits.[5]

The Indians generally tried to protect the free blacks related to them by blood[6] but often stood by when slave hunters took others. Since the Indians cared little for the blacks not related to them, unscrupulous men often abetted slave hunters by selling them fraudulent titles to the blacks or by apprehending the blacks themselves.[7]

The Indians determined the restrictions under which blacks were permitted to reside in the nations. When free blacks applied to the agents for permits to enter the territory, they were refused because they did not come under the Intercourse Law then in force. Without legal guidelines, officials were left to their discretion concerning the protection they could extend to free blacks. James McKissick, the Cherokee agent, put it as follows, and his logic seems to be that applied by military officers at Fort Gibson: "But most certainly in cases when persons of color are permitted to reside in the Indian country they have a just right to claim protection both as to their person and property and if the authorities of the nation give this privilege of residence, and withhold the protection, who is to offer relief? I am of the opinion that the authorities of the Military department partake more of executive discretion."[8]

During the summer of 1854, William Houser, an attorney at Van Buren, Arkansas visited Tahlequah, the Cherokee capital, and offered blacks for sale. It happened that Samuel A. Worcester, a missionary in the Cherokee Nation, was in town and recognized the black family, having at one time hired one of the men as a free hired man. Worcester knew that the Beams family of Choctaw descent had been recognized as free blacks, so he went to the principal chief of the Cherokees; but the chief refused to interfere. Then he went to the Cherokee agent who said that he would not interfere, but he told Worcester that he or anyone else could sue for the freedom of the Beams family in Van Buren. Worcester was not satisfied. Believing the Beams family to be free, he complained to Jefferson Davis and asked for an investigation. Davis denied having given any order in relation to the Beams family except to instruct the military officers to aid the civil authorities in the execution of the law if it became necessary. He wrote, "I abhor any act which deprives a Freeman of his rights and perverts a constitutional law to such base purposes."[9]

Meanwhile, the situation of the captured members of the Beams family had become more desperate, except for David who escaped enroute to Van Buren and returned to the Creek Nation. Houser and his associates had told the blacks and the officers who had helped capture them that the blacks would have a fair and impartial hearing concerning their claims to freedom upon reaching Van Buren. But once there, they found Davis waiting for them and decided to divide the property. Woosly, a slave trader at Van Buren, claimed a fourth interest and took Ellen and

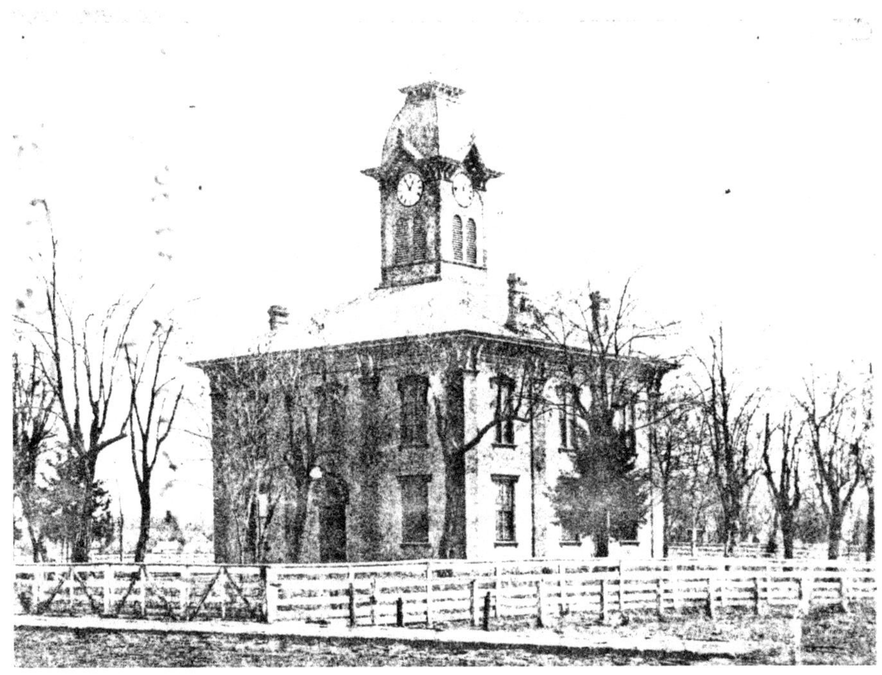

Captured free Beams family members were brought to Van Buren, Arkansas, by slave traders who left before authorities at the Crawford County Courthouse could intervene. *UAFS-Cobb Collection.*

Silas, buying Davis's claim to them. Houser took Martin and William. He sold Martin to Phineas H. White and Thomas B. Emerson, business partners at Van Buren, paying Davis his share of the proceeds, and sold William down the Arkansas River, beyond the jurisdiction of the Circuit Court at Van Buren. Bishop took Mary and her daughter Katy and paid Davis his share.[10]

Worcester's complaint resulted in a demand upon the Superintendent of Indian Affairs at Fort Smith whose files proved the freedom due the Beams family. When the cases went to the jury in 1856, the verdicts were rendered immediately in favor of the Beams family. It was not until late 1858 that all accounts were settled in relation to the Beams family. Their struggle was typical in view of the anomalous position free blacks occupied in the Indian Territory. It was also typical in that their condition was aggravated by political pressures brought to bear on officials by prominent white Southerners, as well as by the bureaucratic incompetence and pro-slavery attitude of many governmental officials in the Indian country.

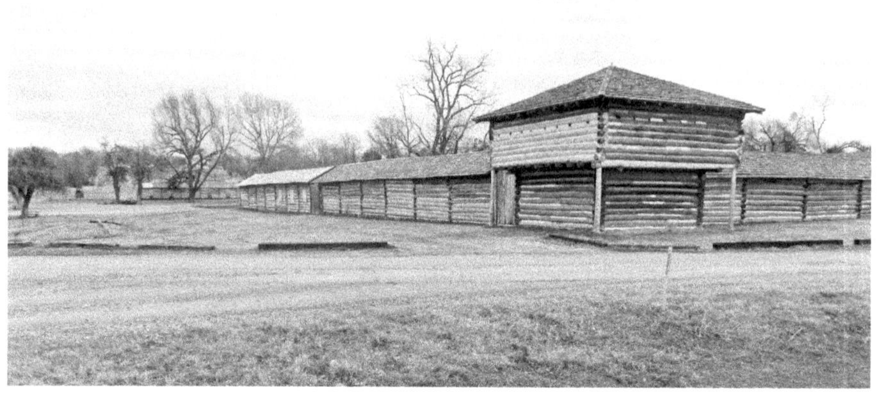

Established in 1824 to keep peace in Indian Territory, Fort Gibson grew (note the buildings beyond) and became a haven for freed slaves. *Jim Roaix.*

However, the outcome of the Beams case was remarkable in light of the temper of the times. As the controversy over slavery gained momentum, most of the Indians became more openly opposed to the existence of enclaves of free blacks in the territory. The Creeks were especially opposed to the blacks on the military reservation at Fort Gibson, who they said exercised "a most pernicious influence" on the slave population and on the more ignorant class of Indians.[11] As demonstrated above, legislation against free blacks became progressively more stringent in most tribes.

In the early summer of 1856, a number of Arkansans made plans to form a company to buy up claims to blacks in the Indian Territory. They would buy claims to free blacks as well as slaves. One of their members bought a claim to a family of free blacks who had lived in the Indian country for years. Only efforts by influential friends kept the purchaser from trying to enforce his claim. Superintendent of Indian Affairs Charles W. Dean feared that unless the government took a hand in controlling slave hunting in the Indian Territory, the peace of the frontier would be jeopardized.[12] To some observers the legal decision in the Beams case was a landmark. As one contemporary put it, the issue of the case was "considered by legal men the more important as the vigorous manner in which it was prosecuted has put a stop to an extensive system of kidnapping, which was in contemplation along the Indian border."[13]

By that time, however, many free blacks, including some members of the Beams family, had fallen victims to the hunters and had been sold as slaves. Others had been killed. For them, the precedent had come too late.

References

1. William G. McLoughlin, "Red Indians, Black Slavery, and White Racism: America's Slaveholding Indians," *American Quarterly* 26 (October 1974): 367–69.
2. Ibid., 381; William G. McLoughlin, "The Choctaw Slave Burning: A Crisis in Mission Work Among the Indians," *Journal of the West* 13 (January 1974): 113–25. See also Grant Foreman, *The Five Civilized Tribes* (Norman: University of Oklahoma Press, 1934), 54, 83, 420.
3. Kenneth W. Porter, *The Negro on the American Frontier* (New York: Arno Press, 1971), 109; Foreman, *Five Civilized Tribes*, 419; McLoughlin, "Red Indians, Black Slavery," 388–81; R. Halliburton Jr., "Origins of Black Slavery Among the Cherokees," *Chronicles of Oklahoma* 52 (Winter 1974–75): 496.
4. *Laws of the Cherokee Nation: Adopted by the Council at Various Periods* (Tahlequah, OK: Cherokee Advocate Office, 1852), 7, 19, 44, 53, 55–56, 71, 173–74, 381; James W. Duncan, "Interesting Ante-Bellum Laws of the Cherokees, New Oklahoma History," *Chronicles of Oklahoma* 6 (June 1928): 179; J.B. Davis, "Slavery in the Cherokee Nation," *Chronicles of Oklahoma* 11 (December 1933): 1,066–67.
5. Many free blacks from time to time sought refuge in the military reservation at Fort Gibson, where the army extended protection to them from slave hunters, who often entered the territory to capture them, or from the Indians, who would capture them and sell them to slave buyers from the states. See National Archives Record Group 393, Fort Gibson, "Indian Affairs," 31, 32; James McKissick to Colonel Gustavus Loomis, July 12, 1847, and Lieutenant F.F. Flint to Captain W.S. Ketchum, September 4, 1848, Gibson Letters Received, Box 3.
6. A good example is the kidnapping of the granddaughters of Shoe Boot, a Cherokee, in 1847. Shoe Boot, whose white wife had left him, married his black servant by whom he had two children. Shoe Boot petitioned for and got free status for his family from the council. When his granddaughters were stolen near Fort Gibson, Charles Landrum and Pigeon Half Breed pursued their captors into Missouri and recovered the free blacks. The National Council not only sanctioned their action but also reimbursed them for their expenses. See Halliburton, "Origins of Black Slavery," 495; *Laws of the Cherokee Nation*, 156; Foreman, *Five Civilized Tribes*, 393.
7. The Creeks were particularly adept at this, as is demonstrated by the slave raids of the 1850s. See, for example, Charles W. Dean to Manypenny, April 29, 1856, M234-802, D153-56, National Archives Record Group 75.

8. McKissick to Loomis, July 12, 1847, Gibson LR, Box 3.
9. Worcester to Davis, September 6, 1854; Butler to Charles E. Mix, November 22, 1854; Davis to Worcester, October 7, 1854, M574-75, Choctaw I727-54, Cherokee B463-54 and Choctaw I272-54.
10. Kingsbury and Folsom to Manypenny, November 20, 1854, and a list of members of Beams family, M574-75, Choctaw K59-54 and C1110-54.
11. B. Marshall et al. to W. Medill, April 6, 1848, M234-228 and M210-48.
12. Dean to Manypenny, June 24, 1856, M234-802 and D180.56.
13. Kingsbury to Manypenny, March 12, 1857, M574-75 and Choctaw C864-57.

CHAPTER 4

FINDING FREEDOM IN FOREIGN LANDS

HENRY BIBB AND THE ABRAHAM MOORE FAMILY

Karen Coody Cooper

Black abolitionist Marcus Garvey, believing that blacks in America would never be treated as equals, became a champion for the creation of Liberia, a new nation carved out of Africa where freed slaves could return to the continent of their ancestral origin. The capital of Liberia was named Monrovia after U.S. President James Monroe. The first of the new settlers began arriving there in 1821.

The family of Abraham Moore, enslaved in the Cherokee Nation, dreamed of moving to Africa. To that end, Abraham and his wife, Nancy, were aided by the mission at Brainerd. We don't know who sold or lent them to the mission, but once there, they were paid wages, money that could be retained by the Moores and used to purchase their freedom. While they engaged in earning and saving money to make the purchase of themselves and a son, their daughter, Violet, also saved and paid for her liberation. The couple's youngest son, John, eight years old, was born after they had achieved freedom. During his early childhood, the family worked to set aside money for the journey. They would have to travel to New Orleans in order to embark for Africa.

Reverend Samuel Worcester wrote in 1853 of the family in *Missionary Herald*, "In 1839, having removed to this side of the Mississippi, they [the Moores] were received into the church at this place, and they have adorned the Christian profession."

The family's success in gaining freedom was due, in part, to a friendly owner allowing the Moores to earn and keep money. Many others with the same dream would never have been able to realize aspirations of purchasing freedom due to experiencing overwork and confinement. The five members of the Moore family all knew how to read, and the youngest child could write, which again shows uncommon indulgence since it was illegal to provide education for slaves.

Worcester wrote, "For the sake of finding a better home for some of their children, they set out in their old age for Liberia, with one son who was born free, one whom they had redeemed, and a daughter whom they had helped redeem."

The ship sailing to Monrovia was named the *Zebra* and left New Orleans on December 31, 1852, with twenty-three freeborn blacks, ninety-seven freed slaves and fifteen who had purchased their freedom. There must have been a jubilant celebration on board as the boat slipped away from its dock. Little would have been known of this journey if tragedy had not occurred to bring it to public notice.

Only a few days into the voyage, improperly cured water barrels led to an outbreak of cholera, and thirty-five emigrants along with the captain, the first mate and three crewmen died. The only surviving member of the Moore family was eight-year-old John, who had lost his entire family and must have been terrified to find himself without loved ones to protect him at such a tender age.

The shipping company denied having defective water, but no other cause was mentioned in the examination of facts following the incident. Young John arrived in Monrovia in March. Nothing further is known of him.

News of the tragedy did reach the Cherokee Nation, and Worcester wrote of the incident in the *Missionary Herald*. The March 16, 1853 *Cherokee Advocate* published the following: "Died at sea, in the month of January last, Abraham Moore and his wife, Nancy, their daughter Violet and their son Charles, free black people, on the way from the Cherokee Nation to the Republic Liberia. Abraham and Nancy had been for many years exemplary professors of religion, and at the time of their departure, were members of the Mission Church at Park Hill." The laudatory announcement rings of regret for the loss of a fine family.

The adventures of Henry Bibb end with a happier conclusion, although his travels did not take him so far or to such an exotic location. However, he did leave his place of slavery in the Cherokee Nation and made his way to Canada in order to be free.

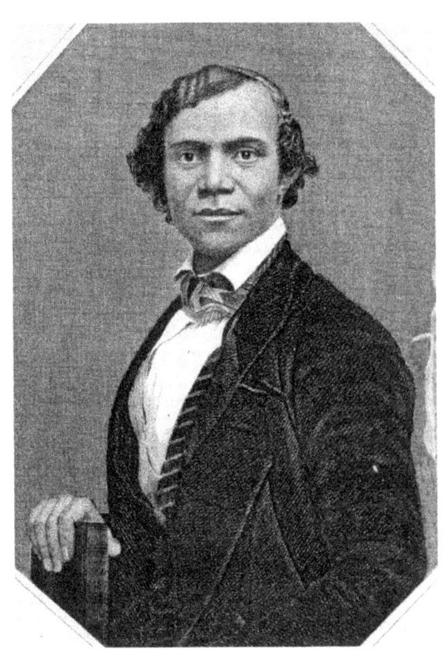

Abolitionist Henry Bibb spent time as a slave in the Cherokee Nation and wrote about his experiences in a published narrative. *Eastern Carolina University.*

Bibb, born in 1815, wrote about his enslaved life and of his escapades seeking freedom. The account was published in New York in 1849 under the title *Narrative of the Life and Adventures of Henry Bibb, an American Slave*, and the booklet has been reprinted. He ran away from owners or captors half a dozen times and was often recaptured while returning in hopes of securing the liberty of his wife and young daughter. He suffered greatly each time he was recaptured, while his wife and child suffered each time he escaped. Ultimately, he gained freedom but was unable to save his family, which served to haunt him throughout the remainder of his life.

Bibb had been born in Kentucky, and his owner was his sire. His mother had been light-skinned from the same situation. Bibb was so light-skinned that he could sometimes pass as a white man. During his first escape from Kentucky, he became familiar with Ohio landmarks and learned about the Underground Railroad. Escaping and being recaptured, it became obvious to his owner that Bibb needed to be sent farther south; as canny as Bibb was, the owner no longer wanted Bibb's wife and daughter for fear Bibb would succeed in helping them escape, so the whole family was sent south. Bibb looked for every opportunity to escape and did manage to get away briefly. The slave buyer/seller found that he could not sell the family in New Orleans since Bibb was known as a runaway. Bibb was told to find himself an owner if he wanted to keep his family together, and so he spent many days along the wharves until he found a Baptist deacon. Thinking that the man would make a fair owner, the family found themselves disappointed with their new situation on the Red River, suffering beatings for minor infractions. The family briefly escaped and suffered terribly when captured. Later, Bibb escaped and was captured by a few men who became his new owners. Being slave sellers, but sympathetic to Bibb, the men tried to purchase Bibb's wife and child, but the cruel deacon would not sell her for any price. So, Bibb was taken to Fayetteville, Arkansas, and his handlers entered Indian Territory and sold Bibb early in 1841 to a wealthy Cherokee man, unnamed in Bibb's account. Bibb was advised by his sellers that he could easily escape from his new owner.

Although Bibb named all his other owners before his last owner, he declined to name his Cherokee owner, perhaps because that family would legally still have last claim of ownership. Bibb did note when he was discussing the religions of his owners that he thought the Cherokee man was Presbyterian. He wrote the following:

> *The same afternoon that the Indian bought me, he started with me to his residence, which was fifty or sixty miles distant. And so great was his confidence in me, that he entrusted me to carry his money. The amount must have been at least five hundred dollars, which was all in gold and silver; and when we stopped over night the money and the horses were all left in my charge.*
>
> *It would have been a very easy matter for me to have taken one of the best horses, with the money, and run off. And the temptation was truly great to a man like myself, who was watching for the earliest opportunity to escape; and I felt confident that I should never have a better opportunity to escape full handed than then.*

Bibb continued:

> *The next morning I went home with my new master; and by the way it is only doing justice to the dead to say, that he was the most reasonable and humane slaveholder that I have ever belonged to.*
>
> *He was the owner of a large plantation and quite a number of slaves. He raised corn and wheat for his own consumption only. There was no cotton, tobacco, or anything of the kind produced among them for market.... The Indians allow their slaves enough to eat and wear....So far as religious instruction is concerned, they have it on terms of equality, the bond and the free....Neither do they separate husband and wives, nor parents and children. All things considered, if I must be a slave, I had by far, rather be a slave to an Indian, than to a white man, from the experience I have had with both.*

Bibb concluded:

> *My last owner was in a declining state of health when he bought me; and not long after he bought me he went off forty or fifty miles from home to be doctored by an Indian doctor, accompanied by his wife. I was taken along also to drive the carriage and to wait upon him during his sickness. But he was then so feeble, that his life was of but short duration after the doctor commenced on him.*
>
> *While he lived, I waited on him according to the best of my ability. I watched over him night and day until he died, and even prepared his body for the tomb, before I left him. He died about midnight and I understood from his friends that he was not to be buried until the second day after his death. I pretended to be taking on at a great rate about his death, but I was more excited about running away, than I was about that, and before daylight the next morning I proved it, for I was on my way to Canada.*

And so, Bibb, with the widow distracted with funeral plans, was able to go unnoticed for a few days, allowing him to gain distance enough to succeed in his escape to Canada. He never recovered his enslaved family, later receiving word that his enslaved wife had formed a new relationship with an owner, and so Bibb himself eventually took another wife as a free man.

References

American Colonization Society 29. "Sailing of the Brig Zebra" (1853): 63–71. The African Repository, Washington, D.C.

Bibb, Henry. *Narrative of the Life and Adventures of Henry Bibb, an American Slave.* N.p.: New York, 1849.

Krauthamer, Barbara. *Black Slaves, Indian Masters: Slavery, Emancipation, and Citizenship in the Native American South.* Chapel Hill: University of North Carolina Press, 2013.

Perdue, Theda. *Slavery and the Evolution of Cherokee Society, 1540–1866.* Knoxville: University of Tennessee Press, 1979.

CHAPTER 5

THE FORTUNATE AND UNFORTUNATE CHILDREN OF SHOE BOOTS

Tiya Miles

The following consists of excerpted portions from Ties that Bind: The Story of an Afro-Cherokee Family in Slavery and Freedom *by Tiya Miles, published by the University of California Press in 2005 and used with permission of author and publisher.*

In 1824, when Captain Shoe Boots submitted a petition to the Cherokee national government on behalf of his enslaved children, his action represented a radical challenge to the emerging Cherokee systems of black exclusion and legalized slavery. Shoe Boots' letter to the General Council acknowledged the intimate relationship between him (a Cherokee citizen) and Doll (his slave), named the children of their union, and pleaded for the children's emancipation and Cherokee citizenship. By writing this letter Shoe Boots made himself vulnerable to the criticism of his fellow slaveholders, including his neighbors Major Ridge, John Ridge, and Joseph Vann, who held key positions on the General Council. Though these men may have engaged in secret liaisons with their own slaves, by 1824 miscegenation between Cherokees and blacks was a shameful and soon to be illegal activity. In his petition, Shoe Boots stated the following:

To your excellencies the Chiefs in council at New Town

My friends and Brothers
It is to you I make my difficulties known, desiring your aid and assistance, knowing it is in your power to give full sanction to this my request. I will here try to give you a full statement; being in possession of a few Black People and being crost in my affections, I debased myself and took one of my black women by the name of Doll, by her I have had these children named as follows, the oldest Elizabeth about the age of Seventeen, the next the name of John about the age of Eleven, the next the name of Polly about the age of Seven years.

These is the only Children I have as Citizens of this Nation, and as the time I may be called on to die is uncertain, My desire is to have them as free citizens of this nation. Knowing what property I may have, is to be divided amongst the Best of my friends, how can I think of them having bone of my bone and flesh of my flesh to be called their property, and this by my imprudent conduct, and for them and their offspring to suffer for generations yet unborn, is a thought of too great a magnitude for me to remain silent any longer.

I therefore humbly petition your honors that you may pass a resolution privileging now to carry into execution my desires, or so direct me by your wisdom, a plea for their freedom, in whatsoever means you may think best.

This your humble petitioner with every prayer of
Captain Shoe Boots[1]

On November 18, 1824, the Council answered Shoe Boots's petition as follows:

The National Council has taken into consideration the petition of Captain Shoe Boots, purporting to grant freedom to his three children which he had by his slave, the Council therefore has no objections to recognizing their freedom, as well as their inheritance to the Cherokee Country.

But it be ordered that Capt. Shoe Boots cease begetting any more Children by his said slave woman provided the National Committee will concur in this decision.

Concurred by the National Committee.[2]

In vehemently forbidding the continuation of the sexual relationship, the Council indicates in no uncertain terms the seriousness of Shoe Boots's transgression. The statesmen seem to have used the occasion of Shoe Boots's petition as an opportunity to publicize its contempt for black and Cherokee "race missing" and to single out black womanhood as a lowly identity; but despite their disapproval, the General Council members capitulated to Shoe Boots's request. The government's favorable response was in no small part due to the Council members' regard for Shoe Boots as a fellow warrior and local leader, but just as important was their shared respect for kinship responsibilities.

They did not, however, wish to continue granting citizenship to black slaves, even those of Cherokee ancestry. In an attempt to foreclose future possibilities for Cherokee and black "intermarriage" that might place them in a similarly awkward position, the General Council passed the following act on November 11, 1824, three weeks after receiving Shoe Boots's petition and one week before ruling on it:

> *Intermarriages between negro slaves and Indians, or whites, shall not be lawful, and any person or persons, permitting and approbating his, her or their negro slaves to intermarry with Indians or whites, he she or they, so offending, shall pay a fine of fifty dollars, one half for the benefit of the Cherokee Nation; and…any male Indian or white man marrying a negro woman slave, he or they shall be punished with fifty-nine stripes on the bare back, and any Indian or white woman, marrying a negro slave, shall be punished with twenty-five stripes on her or their bare back.*[3]

The children were granted Cherokee citizenship not through the recognition of matrilineal descent but through the recognition of their Cherokee patrilineal descent. As it happened, the same body of laws that had narrowed the definition of Cherokee citizenship when it came to black people had broadened that definition when it came to patrilineality. In a revision of matrilineal kinship norms, the Cherokee Constitution included the children of Cherokee men and nonblack, free women as members of the Nation. This shift in legal categorization, together with Shoe Boots's assertion of a kinship of the bone (or father as kin to child), converged to benefit his offspring. The children of Shoe Boots and Doll slid into citizenship through a loophole within a loophole, claiming a right to Cherokee belonging at the crossroads of culture change.

Shoe Boots hoped to protect his offspring in the event of his death by appealing to the General Council for their freedom. And five years after altering

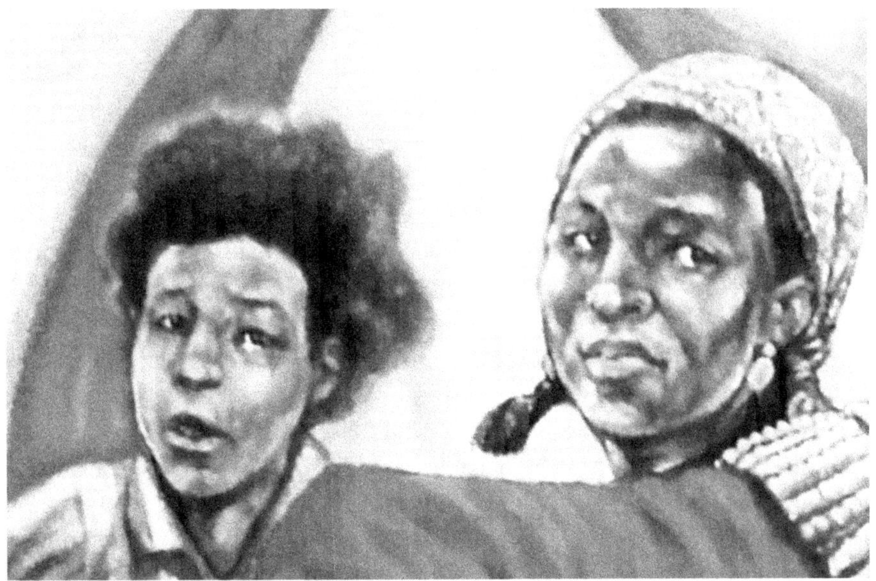

Doll Shoeboots found the status of herself and some of her children threatened following the death of her Cherokee husband. *Dan HorseChief.*

the course of his children's lives, Shoe Boots did die, "at the Thompson Ferry on the Hightower River." The announcement of his passing was published in the *Cherokee Phoenix* newspaper on November 11, 1829 by John Ridge and Thomas Woodward, a mixed-race Cherokee of white ancestry and a nephew of Shoe Boots.[4] As executors of Shoe Boots's estate, Ridge and Woodard announced the procedure for all claims and debts: "Notice, To all whom it may concern, that, the undersigned having been appointed Administrators on the estate of Shoe Boos deceased, we hereby notify all persons indebted to the estate to come forward and make payment, and all persons having claims against the estate to present them for payment within twelve months."[5]

Shoe Boots's three eldest children were legally free and no longer considered part of their deceased father's estate, but the mother was still enslaved, as were the newest additions to their family, little (twin) brothers William and Lewis, who had been born just a few years earlier. Because these two boys had not been listed in Shoe Boots's petition of 1824, they were not protected by the Council's act of emancipation and citizenship. And so it seemed that the fate Shoe Boots had feared for his eldest children, that they would be "divided among the Best of [his] friends," could befall instead his youngest sons.[6]

[T]he Cherokee legislature's proceedings on the twins' case lists only two people as the initiators of the freedom suit: Shoe Boots's two sisters, Peggy and Takesteskee.[7] At least one, and possibly both of them, lived on Shoe Boots's farm and would likely have worked with Doll ever since her arrival thirty years prior. The sisters would also have known their brother's children well and would have seen William and Lewis grow from infants to boys of approximately five to six years—their age at Shoe Boots's death. Beyond the real likelihood of loving attachment between the aunts and their young nephews, Peggy and Takesteskee's willingness to act on behalf of their brother's children would have been in accordance with Cherokee cultural understandings. Brothers and sisters shared an extremely close tie in Cherokee families. The kinship responsibilities between paternal aunts and their nieces and nephews were therefore strong; in the absence of the father, it became the duty of his sisters to protect his children.

The moment when the aunts petitioned the Cherokee government to free their young nephews is one of the most arresting in this family's saga. Not only did three women cross boundaries of race and caste to work together in an imminent crisis, but they also brought what they knew would be an unpopular issue to a governing body controlled by male slaveholders. In a period when Cherokee women had circumscribed political power and black people had none at all, it is remarkable that Peggy, Takesteskee, and Doll almost succeeded in their attempt. The National Council voted to free the boys, but the National Committee refused to concur. It may not surprise that the town-elected National Council supported the request while the small, select governing body of the National Committee rejected it. The National Committee wrote in their succinct response: "The Petition of Peggy and Ta, ke, ste, skee—sisters of the late Capt. Shoe Boots, of High Tower, praying the General Committee to grant the freedom of two boys, Billy and Lewis, said to be children of the said Capt. Shoe Boot, by a black woman of his, and granted by the Council, was received and read. After some enquiry and remarks by the members, the question was taken whether the house should concur with the Council and decided in the negative."[8] Though the Committee's rejection does not detail the content of their "enquiry and remarks" or the reasoning behind their decision, it seems likely that they considered their 1824 order that Shoe Boots end the affair with Doll and their 1824 law outlawing Cherokee-black intermarriage fair warning of their views.

The legal emancipation of Elizabeth, John, and Polly had been a tribal action, sanctioned and preserved by the Cherokee national government. But in 1829 the episode that has been called the first gold rush in American history erupted in Cherokee country. After the discovery of gold in Cherokee territory, the governor of Georgia, already incensed at the Cherokee adoption of a constitution, made the unprecedented move of extending Georgia's legal jurisdiction over the Cherokee Nation and annulling all Cherokee laws. As far as Georgia was concerned, the Cherokee government no longer existed, and the Cherokee people were subject to the mandates of the southern state.

For the marauding Georgians…all blacks were fair game, whether they were slaves, free, or Cherokee citizens. In the early summer of 1830, Elizabeth, Polly, John and their mother, Doll, found themselves running for their lives as Georgia guardsmen hunted them down. On June 12 of that year, the *Cherokee Phoenix* reported: "We are told three Georgia officers were the other day about Hightower, hunting some negroes.…A forged deed of gift is the foundation of the claim.…The emancipated children were kidnapped and taken to Georgia. One of them {John} escaped, but the rest remained in the clutches of the Adventurer."[9] William and Lewis, who had gone to live with Peggy and Takesteskee, were said to be the slaves of the aunts who had tried to free them.[10]

At the end of 1830 Doll and her daughters were living among the slave population in Georgia, and their future looked bleak. The girls had lost their freedom. Doll had lost the relative security that being Shoe Boots's "wife" had afforded her, and all three had lost contact with the boys in the family. John had run away from his would-be captor, and the twins, who had once seemed safe with their aunts, were now separated as well. At the age of sixty-seven William Shoeboots would recall that he was separated from his elder siblings and that his twin brother was snatched away from him, never to be seen again: "Lewis, my brother, had been stolen and carried off. I don't know what ever became of him after that."[11]

Thomas Woodard, Shoe Boots's own nephew, chose to define Doll and the children as property rather than kin. He acquired his cousin Elizabeth… and later sold her to another Georgia citizen.…He also obtained possession of little William, one of the twins.[12]

Elizabeth, now a mother, had passed through the hands of three masters, two of them white, one of them Cherokee. She was a slave for nearly five years before William Thompson (a missionary blacksmith) was able to secure her freedom. By February 1837, Thompson had reached an agreement with her owner to purchase Elizabeth, called Lizza, and her small child for the price of $2,000. The stated purpose of the agreement was "to put her in possession of her freedom."[13] Meanwhile, Doll and William found themselves back in the Cherokee nation, occupying peculiar positions in the home of John Ridge, the second administrator of Shoe Boots's estate. In the account of a Cherokee man who knew the Ridges, there was a "black woman who boarded with Maj or Jno Ridge by the name of 'Dolly.'" William Shoeboots said of his own history: "I stayed with Jno Ridge after my father died—No others of my brothers or sisters stayed with Mr. Ridge."[14]

Doll seems to have played a role akin to slave in the Ridge household, charged as she was with the care and service of Ridge's elderly mother. A former slave of the Ridges remembered that "the mother of [William] Boots lived with old Mrs. Ridge."[15] Another Cherokee man attested: "I always understood that she [Doll] was a slave of Mrs. Ridges: that was the common report."[16] William, however, seems to have enjoyed a more privileged status in the Ridge home, probably because of his Cherokee parentage, youth, and gender. Those who knew the Ridges did not label William a slave, and his stay with John Ridge was understood to be temporary.[17]

Elizabeth managed to return home, a free woman once again. Despite antimiscegenation laws that did not recognize Afro-Cherokees as Cherokee citizens, Elizabeth seems to have received a warm welcome. The promise that Shoe Boots had obtained from Council members guaranteeing his children's "inheritance of the Cherokee Country" was literally realized, and Elizabeth inherited the family farm.[18]

After her release from bondage in the mid-1830s, Elizabeth Shoeboots sought to restore her ravaged family. She gathered those siblings she could locate and became, according to a Cherokee man who knew her, "the head of the family." In the words of this witness, "Lizzie Boots, Polly Boots, John Boots, {William} Boots the above named family all lived together previous to the emigration."[19] Elizabeth must have visited with her mother and brother William often, since she lived just thirty miles from the Ridge estate. John, who had escaped in 1830, may have lived down the road from Elizabeth. Though John Shoeboots' exact whereabouts are unclear from the records, a man named John is listed in the Cherokee Census of 1835, and described as owning eight acres on the Etowah River in 1836. By this time, John Shoeboots was married to a Cherokee woman called Conmenoula, who was described by an associate and former slave as a "full blood Indian," "dark skinned" with "long black hair." The couple had one child, whom they named Mary. The Shoeboots family continued to grow as Elizabeth married a "full blood" Cherokee man named Ferguson (or Ohkilunah-kah) and had her second child with him.[20]

The beleaguered Shoeboots family, along with many others, made the Trail of Tears journey. Doll went West before her daughters, transported by flatboat and steamship, with Major and Susannah Ridge and their slaves. In 1838 Elizabeth and her sister, Polly, walked the Trail of Tears with their young children and relatives.

The Drennen Roll of 1852…catalogs: "Lizzy Boot, Sally, Lotty, Morrison, Dahsegahyahge" and "Polly Boot, Mireah, Eliza Hammer, Louisa, Lizzy, Mary, Chahwahyoocah."

Elizabeth and Polly, free Cherokee citizens, were likely impoverished and struggling in the West. Like other Cherokees forced to remove, they would have been unable to bring many of their possessions with them and awaited the payment of federal annuities. Meanwhile, their mother, Doll, and younger brother, William, who had not been freed by Shoe Boots or accepted as Cherokee citizens, had their basic needs met while occupying an ambiguous position in the households of Major and John Ridge. William, who had lived with John Ridge since Shoe Boots's death, had also traveled West with him: "I came to this country with the Ridges as did my mother Dolly," said William who was apprenticed to John Ridge's brother-in-law "to learn the carpenters trade" and then to another man "to learn the blacksmith trade." Doll worked as a personal servant to Mrs. Ridge. Their circumstances, though unenviable because of their lack of free choice, would have been materially superior to Elizabeth and Polly's, both of who had children of their own and few resources in those early postremoval years.

During the period of the Cherokee slave revolt, Elizabeth Shoeboots was in her late thirties, residing near the Grand River in the Delaware District, in the northeast portion of the Cherokee Nation West. She had separated from her first husband by this time and was living with a Cherokee man named Morton. She now had four children, Claude, Ailsey, Sally, and Morrison. Her sister, Polly, lived nearby with a Cherokee man named Joe and had at least three children: Maria, Lewis, and Joe.

On October 7 the *Cherokee Advocate* printed an announcement titled:

> *Kidnapping: We have been informed that on Tuesday night of last week, two mulatto children were kidnapped from their mother on the Grand River, and ran off into the State. The children are girls, both free, and of Cherokee mixture, and were taken by three men, two of whom were recognized as white men. The wretches entered the house, enquired of the*

> *mother where her children were, tied them while in bed in her presence and took them off—one of them representing himself as the sheriff of the Delaware District.*

The girls, probably Elizabeth's daughters Ailsey and Sally, or Polly's daughter, Maria, were in the hands of these men for more than a month. During that time, the girls were dragged east into Missouri, where they were then advertised for sale. Once sold, the children were likely to have been enslaved in a southern state like Louisiana, where they might have been forced into the "fancy trade" that favored lighter-skinner black women for sexual slavery and concubinage.

A later issue of the *Advocate* printed the following titled Recovered: We mentioned some time ago that a couple of free mulatto girls were kidnapped at their mother's on Grand River….Mr. Charles Landrum, Sheriff of Delaware District, received information as to the course they had been taken, and set out in pursuit of them in company with a Cherokee and a white man. About twelve miles beyond Warsaw, Missouri, he came upon the two girls at a house at which they had been left for sale and has brought them back to the Nation and restored them to their freedom.

On November 12, 1847, "Be it enacted by the National Council, That the sum of twenty-three dollars….allowed out of the National Treasury for the benefit of Charles Landrum and Pigeon Halfbreed…having been expended by them in pursuing into the state of Missouri and recovering the two grand-daughters of Shoe Boot, deceased, who had been kidnapped on the night of the 27th of September last, from their mother in Delaware District, Cherokee Nation, for the purpose of being sold into slavery."

An elderly woman whose capacity for hard work had diminished over time, Doll was no longer of value to the Ridge estate, and the Ridge family emancipated her following Susannah Ridge's death. At the age of approximately seventy, Doll was free at last.

With her hard-won freedom in hand, Doll went to live with her eldest daughter, Elizabeth, who resided in the Delaware District close to the Ridge estate. In 1852, fourteen years after removal, Elizabeth received her federal reimbursement for property in the East, amounting to $456.25. Her sister, Polly, received an annuity that year as well.[21] Elizabeth and Polly then acquired home sites side by side on the west bank of the Grand River, near the juncture of Honey Creek. Their homesteads are numbered 233 and 234 in an anonymous account book in which Elizabeth's plot is valued at $344.00 and marked "paid," and Polly's plot is valued at $529.75.[22] John

Shoeboots, who had started a family in the East after eluding slavecatchers almost twenty years earlier, had departed from Georgia alone in 1845 and traveled West "to hunt his folks."[23] Soon thereafter, he rejoined his sisters in the Delaware community of the Cherokee Nation West.[24]

In 1852 Doll submitted her application to an Arkansas court, stating that Shoe Boots had been an officer in the Creek War, and she had been his wife. Doll's explanation of her relationship with Shoe Boots must have been convincing to the court since she received a warrant for forty acres of land....By 1858, however, the Missouri court...issued a warrant for one hundred and twenty acres to "Dolly Shoeboots, widow of Shoeboots, a Cherokee Indian."

By 1860 Doll Shoeboots, known also by her Cherokee name, Congeeloh, was a free, propertied woman.[25] A census of free inhabitants living among the Five Tribes of the West lists her as an eighty-year-old "housekeeper" in the Delaware District of the Cherokee Nation. Not long after this census was completed, Doll passed away. She had lived sixty years among Cherokees as a sister outside of that community, linked by relationships, separated by race.

In 1888 William Shoeboots had his day in court and made his case for citizenship. At the age of sixty-four, William may well have been the last surviving child of Shoe Boots and Doll. And like his father before him, William engaged in a public action that challenged the Cherokee Nation's limited definition of the relationship between race and citizenship....William made a statement that reveals a notion of Cherokee-ness based not on racial designation but on family lines and kinship circles.

However, the Cherokee Commission on Citizenship was conflicted in their assessment of William's claim. In their response they expressed that they were bound by an Act of Council to make a determination based not on whether a claimant was Cherokee by kinship but on whether that claimant could trace his or her lineage to particular Cherokee rolls beginning in 1835. Their decision would thus be guided by restrictive governmental codes that were more reflective of a legalistic, even colonial, apparatus than of the complexities of Cherokee relationships. Shoe Boots died in 1829, never making it onto these official rolls. His eldest children, who had been freed and admitted to citizenship by petition, did appear on the census of 1835 (John) and the Drennen roll of 1851 {Elizabeth and Polly}. However, their enrollment was not considered relevant to William's case because they were not his lineal antecedents.

John Cochran, a great-nephew of Shoe Boots, was likely the grandson of Peggy or Takesteskee, the two sisters of Shoe Boots who had once fought for

William and Lewis's freedom before the Cherokee Council. In his statement, Cochran reclaims relational ties that the women in his family had long held dear, offering memories of kinship to mediate the ravages of racial separation. He names Shoe Boots's nation and clan, links Shoe Boots to his own mother, and connects all this information to the births of Shoe Boots and Doll's children. In doing so, Cochran weaves Shoe Boots and his family into a web of familial, clan, and tribal relationships. He indicates, in words both plain and insightful, that long before the Cherokees became a race-conscious nation, Shoe Boots was a Cherokee. And in accordance with the logic of kinship, so too were his children.

References

1. Captain Shoe Boots to the Chiefs in Council, October 20, 1824, Cherokee Nation Papers, roll 46, no. 6508, Western History Collections, University of Oklahoma, Norman, Oklahoma.
2. *Laws of the Cherokee Nation: Adopted by the Council at Various Periods* (Tahlequah, OK: Cherokee Advocate Office, 1852).
3. Ibid.
4. Citizenship Application of William Shoeboots, Dawes Commission; *Cherokee Phoenix*, June 12, 1830.
5. *Cherokee Phoenix*, November 11, 1829.
6. Captain Shoe Boots to the Chiefs in Council, October 20, 1824, Cherokee Nation Papers, roll 46, no. 6508, Western History Collections, University of Oklahoma, Norman, Oklahoma.
7. John Howard Payne Papers, 8:46, 8:64–65, Ayer Collection, Newberry Library, Chicago, Illinois.
8. Ibid.
9. Ibid.
10. William G. McLoughlin, *Cherokee Renascence in the New Republic* (Princeton, NJ: Princeton University Press, 1986), 345.
11. Citizenship Application of William Shoeboots.
12. Ibid.
13. Cherokee Nation Papers, "Agreement to Free Lizza Shoeboots," 46:6512, Western History Collections, University of Oklahoma, Norman, Oklahoma.
14. Citizenship Application of William Shoeboots.
15. Ibid.
16. Ibid.

17. Ibid.
18. Citizenship Application of William Stephens. During the interview and application process, witnesses for people often provided good information about neighbors and people who had traveled with them when establishing time and place regarding themselves, so this is that kind of instance.
19. Citizenship Application of William Shoeboots.
20. Ibid.
21. "True List of the Names of Cherokee Indians Who Have Emigrated," Records of the Cherokee Agency in Tennessee, 1801–35, transcribed by Marybelle W. Chase, 1990, page 48, no. 413.
22. "Anonymous Accounts," 1852, Cherokee Nation Papers, 45:6432.
23. Northern District Citizenship Case Files, Case 32, Mary Swagerty, National Archives Microfilm Publication M7RA-388, roll 3, Oklahoma Historical Society.
24. Citizenship Files, Mary Swagerty, Statement of Benjamin Hawkins.
25. The reference to Doll's Cherokee name comes from her associate, Thomas Ridge, a slave of Major Ridge; Citizenship Application of William Shoeboots, Statement of Thomas Ridge.

CHAPTER 6

STOLEN AWAY AIKY

Celia E. Naylor

Excerpted with permission from African Cherokees in Indian Territory: From Chattel to Citizens *by Celia E. Naylor, published by the University of North Carolina Press in 2008, 67–73.*

A year and a half after the kidnapping of Shoe Boots' granddaughters, on 19 February 1849, the *Cherokee Advocate* reported another case involving the kidnapping of Cherokee freedpeople from the Nation. A lengthy letter dated 16 January 1849 from J.T. Trezevant, mayor of South Memphis, addressed to the editor of the *Cherokee Advocate* provided detailed information regarding the status of two freedwomen who claimed they had been kidnapped from their home in the Cherokee Nation. Mayor Trezevant's letter indicated that the "two Cherokees" were living at his residence. One of the women who had been kidnapped related her story to Cherokee John Brown during his visit to Trezevant's residence in July 1848. Aiky explained that about 25 May 1848, "she and her daughter Nannie were stolen and carried away from Archibald Campbell's by a young man named Chisholm (A.F.) and a negro Spaniard—called Moses. She recalled "that she was knocked down and her hands tied, and she and her daughter put in a canoe—that Chisholm made her lie down in the canoe, whenever they were passing a settlement on the River—that they were brought to Ft. Smith or Little Rock...and then put on a Steam boat and brought to this place to be sold." Although Chisholm held a bill of sale for them it was "doubtless manufactured for the purpose."

When Aiky and Nannie arrived in Memphis, members of the Memphis community requested Trezevant's intervention in their sale, as some citizens "thought there was foul play going on." Although he was uncertain about what actions to take, Trezevant was "convinced from observations, and from signs from the woman, that she was not an Indian Negress." In June 1848 Trezevant, a lawyer by profession, "commenced suit against Chisholm, and upon application, the Judge had her taken out of his custody by the Sheriff, with instructions to place her somewhere." Because "no one would take them," and not wanting them to "go to prison merely for safe keeping," Trezevant took them to his residence, "where they have been ever since." In response to the actions of Trezevant, Chisholm left Memphis and promised "to return with evidence to prove her a slave...but he has not yet come."

Trezevant estimated that the case would be presented in March 1849. Because he did not believe Chisholm would return for them, he thought that the women would be set free again. Trezevant's letter appealed to the Cherokee people to compensate him for the expenses he had incurred in providing for these women. He described the women as a "dead expense," as they did not "know how to do the business or duties of a house servant." Even though he had provided for these women for several months, he thought they were also "in a way—dirty and offensive." If he won the suit, Trezevant requested $500 from the Cherokee Nation to compensate him not only for expenses already paid to provide for the two women but also for their passage home.

In February 1849 James S. Vann, editor of the *Cherokee Advocate*, highlighted the urgency of the freedwomen's situation in a lead article. He supported the veracity of the women's story, emphasizing that the "statements therein made by the women, Aiky and Nannie, are substantially true, so far as we are able to ascertain the facts. Those women were given their freedom by their mistress at her death—of which fact there is indubitable proof in the country. The writer of the will is now living, and is at the present time the high Sheriff of Canadian District.—The witness to the same is also alive—Mr. John Leack of Canadian District....He is well known by most of the citizens of this Nation to be strictly a man of truth."

Vann recalled that two years earlier, in 1847, "there was a Cherokee prosecuted and tried by the authorities of the Nation, for the offence of selling these same free women. But the evidence not being sufficient to prove the fact, he was acquitted of the charge. In this trial and acquittal,

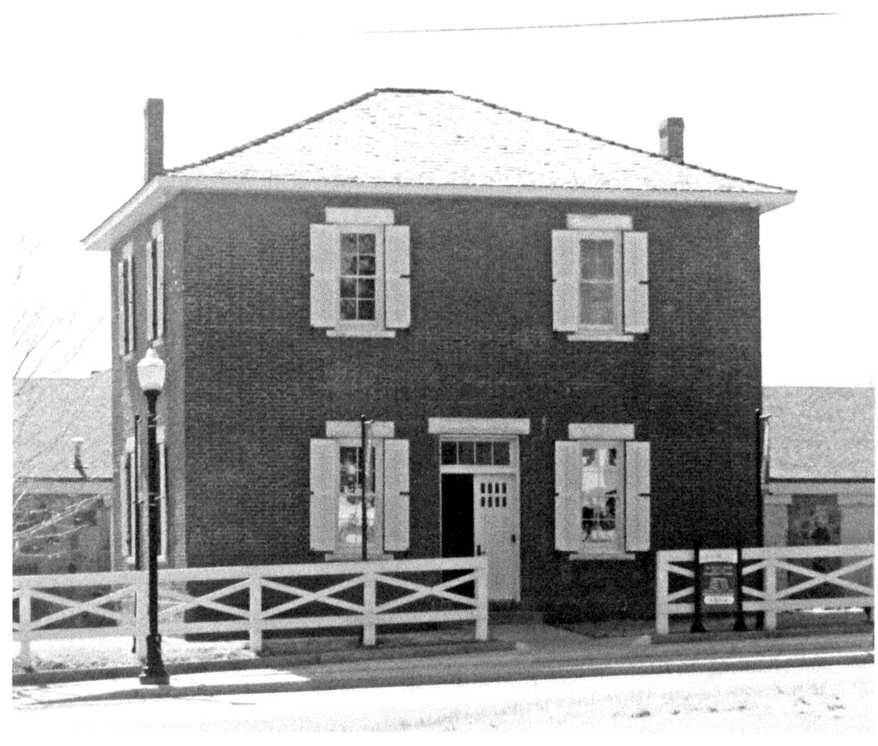

The *Cherokee Advocate* reported on stolen free black citizens; the old press is displayed in the Cherokee Supreme Court Building, built in 1844 in Tahlequah. *Jim Roaix.*

the question of their freedom was not at all involved. That was an acknowledged fact, as well as proven on the day of the trial. The question was not, were these persons free or not—but did the prisoner sell them? The evidence was not sufficient to convict, consequently he was liberated." Having never considered Chisholm "an honorable man," Vann also expressed doubt as to "A.F. Chisholm being the owner, or in any way concerned in the concocting of the bill of sale." Vann believed "*it the duty of the nation to attend to the matter, and extend the same watchful care to these unfortunate women, it has ever intended to their citizens, when placed in unfortunate circumstances.* The magnanimous and philanthropic conduct and aid which the generous Mayor of Memphis has extended to our suffering citizens, should not be passed by in silence. But the most prompt and efficient measures should be taken to aid him in bringing about an act of justice." Vann clearly identified these two women as part of the Cherokee Nation, part of the Cherokee community, part of the Cherokee citizenry. This was not an issue of Cherokee "property" being stolen; it was a matter of two Cherokee citizens being in "unfortunate circumstances" and "suffering" as a result of their freed status being compromised.

Aiky and her family had been plagued with kidnapping attempts. Even while Aiky and her daughter Nannie attempted to regain their freedom while retained in Memphis, Aiky's other two daughters engaged in a legal battle for their own freedom. In her story, Aiky stated that "she had two (other) daughters, Peggy and Betsy," who were stolen in 1847 and sold "by a man named Shore." After they were stolen, "she and Nannie ran in the woods and kept out of the way, until one of the Coodeys, who was a friend of hers got her to go to Arch Campbell's or his sons—to stay, until some suit about her freedom should be decided. While at Campbell's she (Aiky) was stolen, during his absence from home." Peggy and Betsy would finally have their say in court three years later. In October 1850, *Cherokee Advocate* editor David Carter included a notice indicating that the case of Peggy and Betsy, "claiming their freedom, as free-born Cherokees," would be addressed "in the Courts of Judicature, in the State of Mississippi." At the time the notice appeared in the newspaper, those involved with the case were in the Cherokee Nation "procuring what testimony they may be able to gather in reference to the subject." Mr. Wair, "the innocent purchaser of Peggy and Betsy from the Shores, certain negro-traders of the State of Arkansas, having been sued by Peggy and Betsy for their freedom, as well as for damages to the amount of several thousand dollars, is desirous of procuring all the testimony that can be got in the Cherokee country in reference to such fact."

While investigating Peggy and Betsy's story, Wair had "learned that Peggy and Betsy were once owned as slaves by a Cherokee woman named Wut-ty, who set them free by a Will, at her death. Or, that Peggy and Betsy had failed to establish such Will by law, and were consequently held as estate property and sold as slaves." From Mr. Wair's statement, it appeared that he had "no wish whatever, to enslave the said Peggy and Betsy as freed negroes, and much less as free-born Cherokees. But that his sole object is to ascertain whether they are freed negroes or free-born Cherokees." This distinction was particularly important "as the damage in the later case will be a large amount. Whereas in the former it will be but trifling, perhaps only the purchase money and cost of suit."

Editor Carter explained that "the report in this country, so far as we have been able to learn is, that Peggy and Betsy were set free, or intended so to be, by the old Lady Wut-ty, at her death." However, "the said Peggy and Betsy not understanding what would be necessary for them to do in the premises, and not knowing any thing of the formalities of law, and from the sinister motives of those who ought to have instructed them in this matter, they remained in ignorance of their true situation, until since they have been placed in the situation they are now in." Carter noted that "a Mr. Montgomery, a citizen of the State and neighborhood where Peggy and Betsy were sold, in connection with a Mr. Hildebrand, a citizen of this Nation, have undertaken to assist Peggy and Betsy to secure their freedom, by a suit at law in the State where they live." Carter expressed his hope "that those who may know any thing of the matter, will not hesitate to let it be known, in order that the truth may be ascertained." In addition, any person having information on this matter was asked to attend a meeting on 7 October 1850 to provide evidence that would restore Peggy's and Betsy's freedom. Unfortunately, from the extant documents, it is uncertain if Aiky and her daughters ever regained their freedom.

Whether astonishing or expected, the aftereffects of the kidnapping of Shoe Boots's granddaughters unequivocally verified an understanding of free African Cherokees belonging to Cherokee communities. Possible expectations and claims of free biracial African Cherokees, including Shoe Boots's kin, establish some degree of consciousness about their identity as part of the Cherokee Nation—as legitimate members of Cherokee communities. Such claims reflected intertwined realities of bondage and freedom, as well as blood relations between red and black in the antebellum Cherokee Nation.

Though not granted the same rights as Shoe Boots's granddaughters, being neither of Cherokee ancestry nor freeborn Cherokee citizens, Aiky, her daughters, and other Cherokee freedpeople in the Nation may also have developed a similar kind of consciousness about their legitimate place in the Cherokee Nation and expected some degree of protection. Indeed, the Nation's responses to the kidnapping attempts of Aiky and her kin articulated a belief about freedpeople belonging to the Nation—not owned by the Nation. When Aiky and her daughters discovered the actions of free Cherokees to reinstate their freedom, did such dealings mirror their own conceptions of belonging to and being a part of the Cherokee Nation beyond the realm of bondage? While enslaved, they had certainly become familiar with the degrading aspects of bondage. Nevertheless, after their Cherokee mistress manumitted them, they remained within the boundaries of the Cherokee Nation. Their decision to stay after attaining freedom might not have simply occurred as a result of their familiarity with Cherokees; it could have reflected deeply embedded feelings about the Cherokees and the Cherokee Nation as home. Even without blood ties to the Cherokees, Aiky and other recently freed African Cherokees in antebellum Cherokee country believed that they belonged to Cherokee communities not merely because of their previously defined position as chattel owned by Cherokees.

References

Cherokee Advocate, September 9, 1847; January 6, 1848; February 19, 1849; September 18, 1850; October 1, 1850; October 8, 1850. Indian Territory.

CHAPTER 7

115-YEAR-OLD PART NEGRO–PART CHEROKEE WOMAN

With comments by Karen Coody Cooper

Such was the headline on the front page of the June 15, 1903 Coffeyville Daily Journal. *The given name of the individual was wrongly reported (her first name was actually Susan), and the article takes us back to a past journalistic time.*

> *Saturday afternoon Coffeyville had within her gates one of the oldest women in the United States. She does indeed claim the distinction of being the oldest woman in the Indian Territory. She is 115 years old and her name is either Martha Mayhew or Martha Coody; she goes by both names. She lives near Coody's Bluff and is part Negro and part Cherokee Indian. Her visit to this city Saturday was for the purpose of making affidavit before Major A.B. Powell that she is 115 years of age, is a citizen of the Cherokee nation and is unable by reason of her extreme age to go to Muskogee, I.T., for the purpose of taking her allotment. This was done. Old Aunt Martha surely shows her age and there is a copious amount of testimony to show that she is as old as she says she is. The most remarkable thing about her is that she doesn't claim to be a slave of Washington. All the rest of the old colored men or women of the country do. She was brought up from her home in a spring wagon and stood the twenty-mile trip well. She reclined on a cot in the back of the wagon and viewed with much interest the stretches of country traveled. On arriving at Major Powell's office, she had to be lifted down and assisted into the office. She also had to be lifted up and down off her chair when she arose to sign the affidavit. By the way, she didn't "sign"*

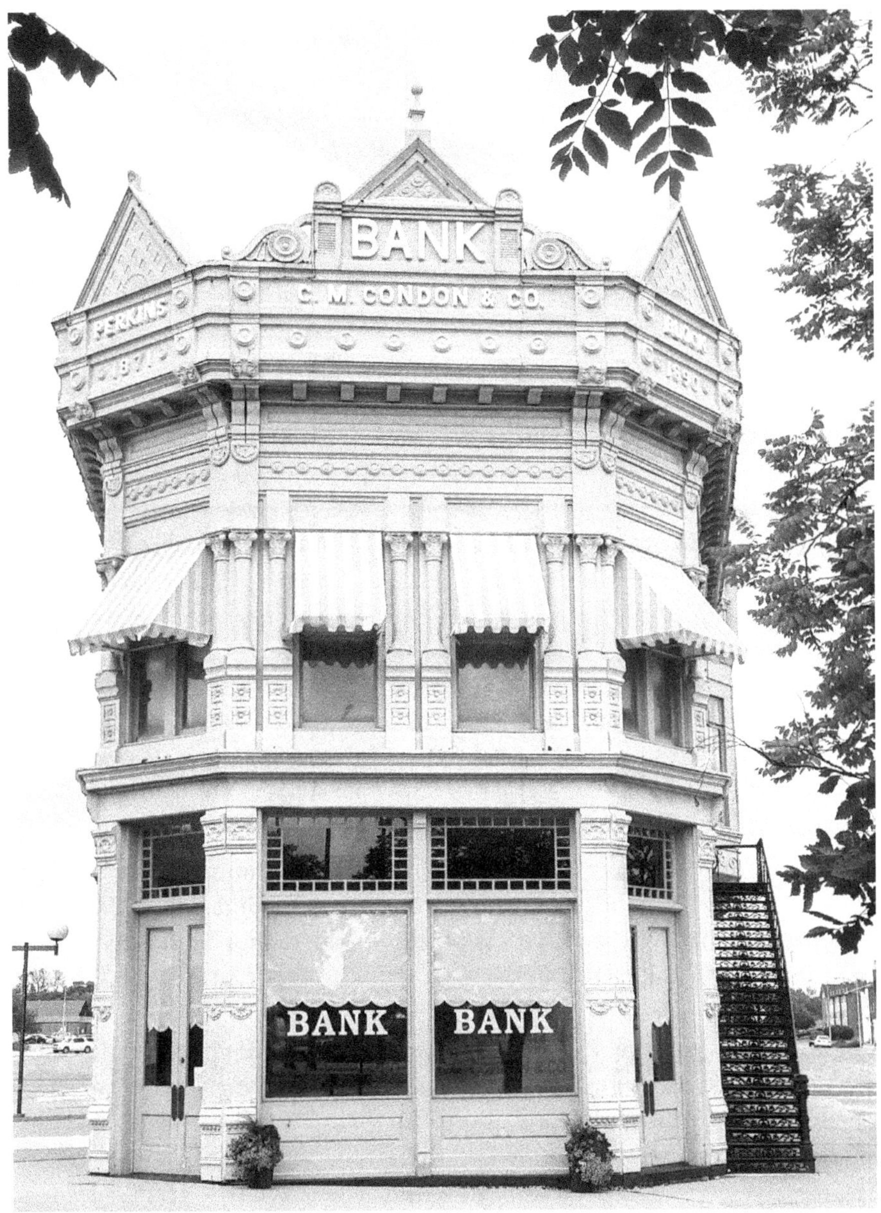

During Susan Mayhew's trip to Coffeyville, Kansas, she probably saw this historic bank, known for being robbed by the Dalton Gang. *Coffeyville Convention & Visitors Bureau.*

> *the paper; she made a wavering uncertain mark. Two of her companions, William Bradford and Roe Vann, witnessed the paper. The affidavit was one put to her for the purpose by the government. Aunt Martha, was she not bowed down with the weight of her years, would be about five feet six inches tall. She is much attenuated, her frail body not weighing over seventy-five pounds. Her kinky hair is white and her gums are, save for a few yellow snags, destitute of teeth. Her tiny black eyes, a little yellowed in the corners, still have some snap and fire in them. She talks in a quavering voice, slowly but plainly. Her hands, drawn and bent with age and rheumatism, are more like the claws of an animal than they are those of human. Her face is ape-like in its aspect and her general appearance is that of a mummy. She was accompanied by a number of old friends, all of whom declared that when they were tiny children, Aunt Martha was then a very old woman. The old lady was a slave for years and years and used to tell many stories of her childhood. Of late years it has been an effort for her to talk much and her memory is beginning to fail, but she is still an Interesting old woman. She has lived in the territory ever since the Cherokees came there from Georgia. She was taken back Saturday evening.*

Interestingly, the same newspaper had previously written about *Susan* Coody on August 4, 1900, noting her to be 111 years old at that time and reporting that she lived eight miles southeast of Coffeyville. That short piece noted that her husband had been "a servant of General Jackson."

Susan Coody's Dawes Commission interview in Nowata in June 1901 requested her age, and she responded, "About a hundred." We learn that she had had children, but no further information about them has been found. Her interview informs us that she had first been a slave of Charles Coody, who was born in 1792 and who had married in 1810 in Roane County, Tennessee. When Charles died in 1844, Susan became the property of his son, Richard (Dick) Coody, although Charles's wife, Ellenor, was still living. Susan never cited who her father was, and she made no documentable claim to Cherokee blood in records.

Charles Coody had been an Old Settler Cherokee who started a farm at Park Hill before Removal. His step-uncle, Joseph Coodey, was married to the eldest sister of Chief John Ross. Charles Coody sold his home to John Ross, providing a base of operations for Ross while the chief oversaw the construction of a more stately home and worked at reestablishing the Cherokee Nation's government. Charles resettled with his family to Nowata, and the area near him became known as Coody's Bluff. Charles served as a district judge and served a term as president of the Cherokee National Council.

Susan and her spouse were transferred to Jacob (Jake) Bushyhead in exchange for a single black male slave. Susan reported that she had then been hired out to missionary Samuel Worcester, who eventually obtained ownership of the elderly couple and allowed them to "work their time out." Susan reported that she and her husband had thus been freed by Worcester.

Worcester, a white minister, learned to temper his antislavery views while ministering to the Cherokees. Elizur Butler noted that Worcester "refuses to employ slave labor unless the slave received wages, thus making a stab at the Institution of Slavery." The few slaves he obtained were known to dine with Worcester's family at the same table, a practice frowned upon by others.

During the Civil War, Susan and her husband took refuge at Fort Scott in Kansas. Sam Webber testified to the return in 1866 of her husband, "Uncle Calbert Maye," and noted that he had immediately returned to Kansas to

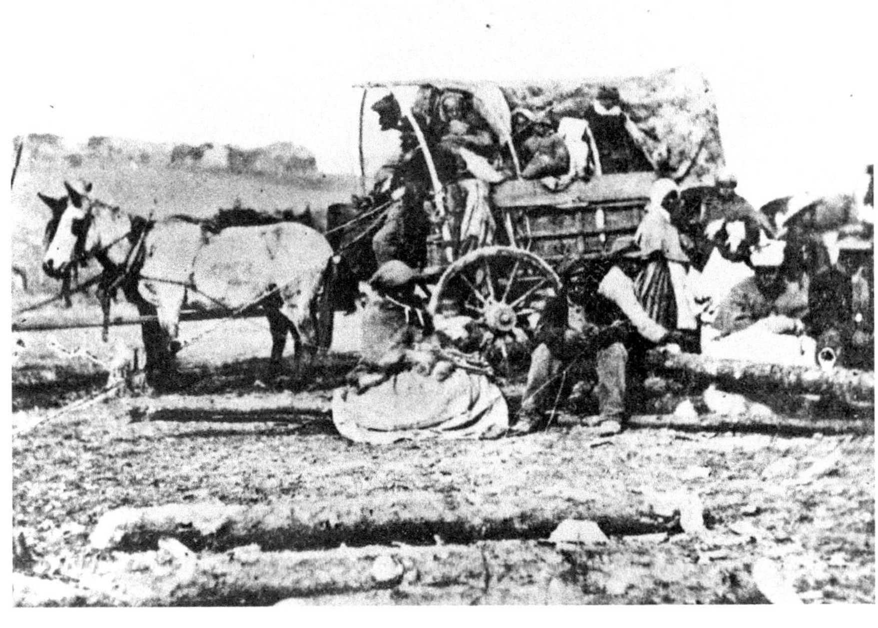

During the Civil War, Indian Territory's free black families and Union Cherokees headed north to Kansas for protection. *National Archives and Records Administration.*

retrieve his wife after making a claim. One witness reported that he and others called Susan "grandmother" as early as the 1840s. The grandson of Charles Coody noted that Susan's husband was called Old Man Colbert or Mayhew. The name Colbert Mahew is found among an 1877 list concerning a lawsuit, *George Wesley Davis v. Cherokee Nation*, which resulted in awarding those on the list a chance to be reassessed regarding previous rejection regarding Freedman enrollment. Nothing further is found about Colbert Mayhew, who possibly died before making reapplication. Interestingly, Ellenor Riley, bride of Charles Coody, had an uncle named George Colbert, so it is likely that Colbert Mahew and his wife, Susan Coody, became linked through their owners' marriage.

What we don't know about Susan is who her children were (she likely outlived them all), nor her date of death or location of burial. Susan was a venerable woman born in the eighteenth century in Georgia, dying in the twentieth century in the Coffeyville area.

CHAPTER 8

CHEROKEE SLAVE REVOLT OF 1842

Art T. Burton

Reprinted with permission

Black slavery in America usually evokes images of the antebellum South, but few realize that members of the Five Civilized Tribes—the Cherokees, Choctaws, Chickasaws, Creeks, and Seminoles—in Indian Territory, today's Oklahoma, also had slaves. Like their counterparts in the South, Indian slaveholders feared slave revolts. Those fears came true in 1842 when slaves in the Cherokee Nation made a daring dash for freedom.

In the 1830s and 1840s, initially at the insistence of President Andrew Jackson, the United States government forcibly removed the Five Civilized Tribes from their homes in Mississippi, Alabama, Tennessee, North Carolina, Georgia, and Florida to Indian Territory west of the Mississippi River. Their removal opened the lands to white settlers and planters.

When they moved, all of the tribes took with them established systems of slavery. Mixed-blood Indians, the offspring of white traders and frontiersmen who married Indian women, were the principal slaveholders in the tribes, largely because their fathers had taught them the economics of slavery. Those mixed-blood Indians remained tribal members and became important middlemen between white settlers and Indian communities.

Many Cherokees depended on black slaves as a bridge to white society. Full-blood Indian slave owners relied on the blacks as English interpreters and translators.

By 1860, the Cherokees had 4,600 slaves; the Choctaws, 2,344; the Creeks, 1,532; the Chickasaws, 975; and the Seminoles, 500. Some Indian slave owners were as harsh and cruel as any white slave master. Indians were often hired to catch runaway slaves; in fact, slave-catching was a lucrative way of life for some Indians, especially the Chickasaws.

Seminoles attitudes toward slavery were different than those of other tribes. Never practicing chattel slavery, they took in fugitive slaves and claimed them as their own "property" to protect the blacks from slave-catchers. In return, the blacks, who lived in separate villages in the Seminole country, gave livestock and crop tributes to the Indians. The blacks and Seminoles also formed a military alliance, with the blacks serving the Indians as warriors and strategists. In some instances, the blacks would intermarry into the Seminole community.

All of the tribes except the Seminoles had slave codes. Even after their removal to Indian Territory, the Seminoles allowed their slaves to carry weapons and own horses and other property. Until a treaty in 1845 provided for their relocation to the western area of the Creek Nation, the Seminoles lived in the Cherokee country around Fort Gibson, Indian Territory. Before that, Cherokee and Creek slaveholders complained about the influence of Seminole slaves on their own slave populations.

The Cherokee slaves at the Arkansas River port of Webbers Falls, not far from Fort Gibson, would have had ample opportunity to observe the Seminole slaves. Most of the Cherokee slaves farmed cotton and other crops, but some worked at the landing where steamboats docked and where Joseph Vann operated a public ferry. The Seminoles disembarked at Webbers Falls after their journey from Florida, and the Cherokee slaves may have been impressed with the blacks dressed in Seminole fashion and carrying rifles and knives. The black Seminoles settled in the Illinois River bottoms near Webbers Falls, allowing the Cherokee slaves to socialize with them regularly.

About 4:00 a.m., November 15, 1842, more than twenty-five slaves, most from Vann's plantation at Webbers Falls, rendezvoused at a prearranged location near the port town. The blacks locked their masters and overseers in their houses and cabins while they slept. Then they burglarized the store of a man named Bigelow, stealing guns, horses, mules, ammunition, food, and supplies. At daylight the group, which included men, women, and children, headed toward Mexico, where slavery was illegal and many runaway slaves sought refuge. When the fugitive slaves entered the Creek Nation southwest of Webbers Falls, slaves from the

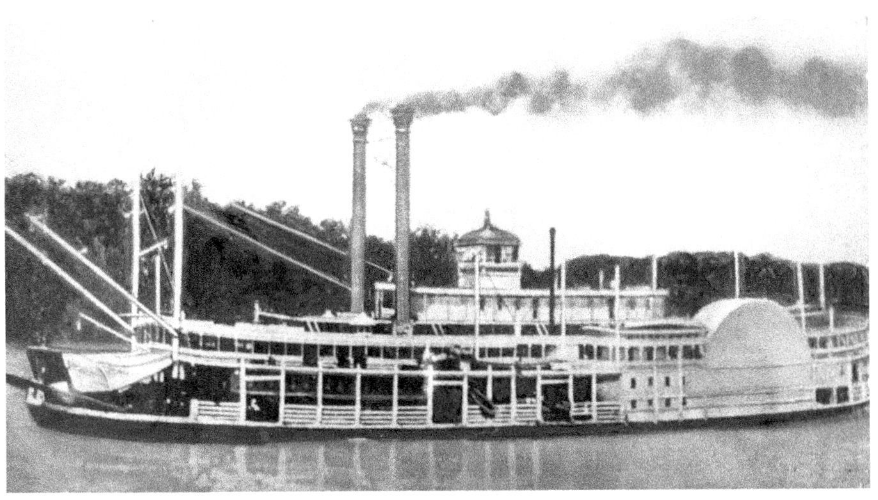

Joe Vann's recaptured slaves resided on his steamship *Lucy Walker*, making escape difficult. In 1843, Vann ordered the boiler stoked so high it exploded, killing most on board. *The Oklahoman Archives.*

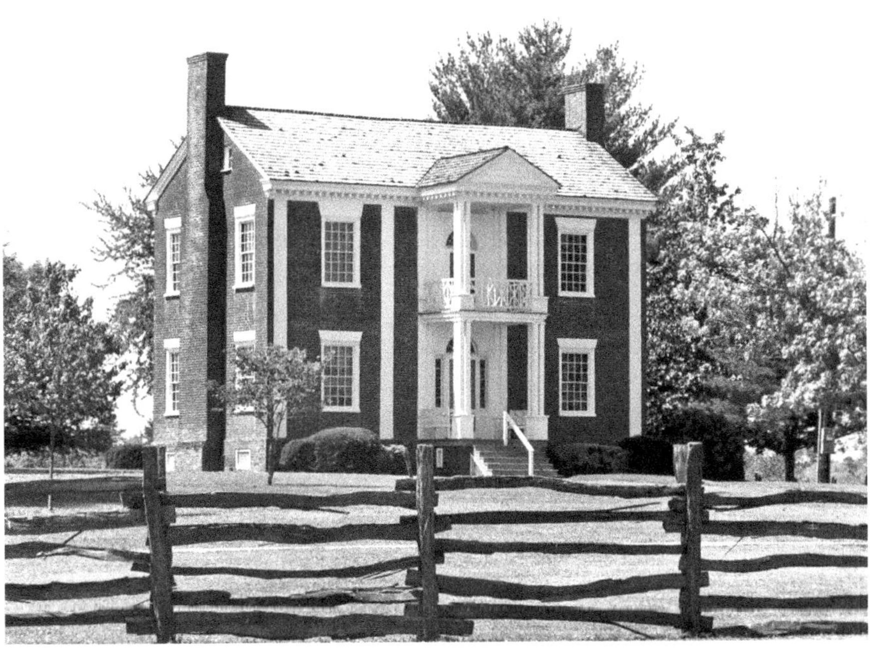

The Vann House in Georgia was duplicated in Webbers Falls by Joseph Vann. The western house survived the slave revolt of 1842 but burned in the Civil War. *Chief Vann House Historic Site in Georgia.*

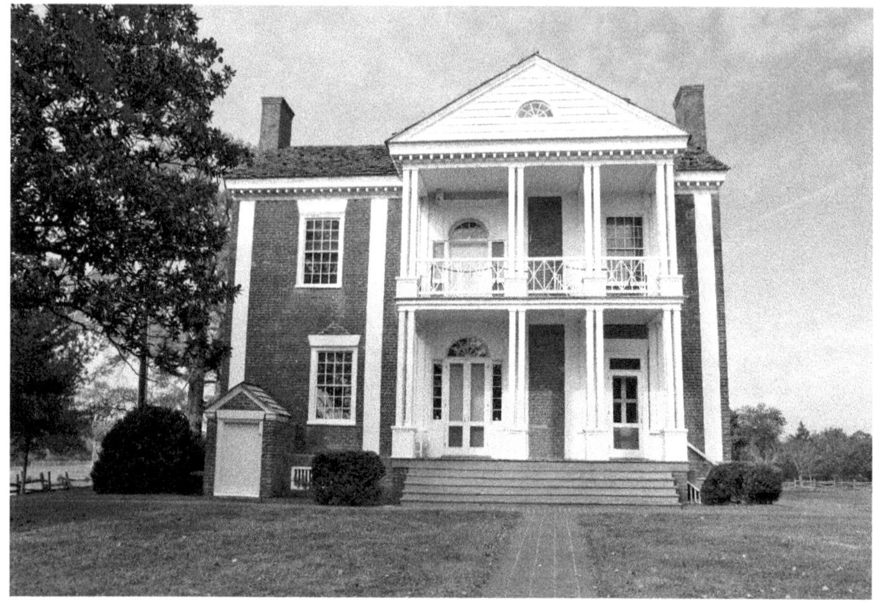

While the front of the Vann House had a formal entrance, the back offered large porches, important for comfort in hot climes. *Chief Vann House Historic Site in Georgia.*

plantations of wealthy Creeks named Bruner and Marshall joined them, increasing the number of runaway to more than thirty-five.

When the Cherokees discovered that their slaves had departed, about forty of them took guns and dogs and went in pursuit of the fugitives. Each slave reportedly had a horse or mule to ride, and they had taken some of Vann's blooded racehorses, so they were highly mobile. The Cherokees followed the slaves into the Creek Nation. There a group of Creek Indians organized a search party and joined the Cherokees.

Within a few days of the escape, the Indians caught up with the blacks about ten miles beyond the Canadian River in the Choctaw Nation. The slaves found a depression in the prairie which provided a complete entrenchment for them and their horses, and they decided it would make an excellent place to fight. A pitched battle followed, with both sides suffering casualties. The blacks held the position for two days, but the Indians killed two of them and captured twelve others.

The fight convinced the Cherokees and Creeks to go home and get reinforcements before continuing the chase. The remaining fugitives kept moving toward the Red River.

During their flight, the fugitives met James Edwards, a white man, and Billy Wilson, a Delaware Indian, about fifteen miles from the battle site. Edwards and Wilson were fugitive slave hunters, whom blacks in the South called patrollers or "patty rollers." They had with them eight blacks—one man, two women, and five children—who had escaped in the Choctaw Nation. They had belonged to a white man named Thompson, who had married a Choctaw woman, making him a citizen of the Choctaw Nation. The fugitives had been headed west to join one of the Plains Indian tribes when a man named Chisholm spotted them and turned them over to Edwards, Wilson, and a Cherokee man for transport back to Choctaw authorities.

Edwards and Wilson made good progress until they met the fugitive Cherokee and Creek slaves, who killed them. The Choctaw blacks gladly joined the Cherokee band as they continued on their journey toward Mexico.

The slave outbreak was reported to the Cherokee National Council at the capital in Tahlequah on November 17, 1842. Immediately the council passed a resolution, which Chief John Ross approved, authorizing Cherokee Militia Captain John Drew to raise a company of one hundred men to pursue, arrest, and deliver the blacks to Fort Gibson. The resolution also relieved the Cherokee Nation of any liability if the slaves resisted arrest and were killed. The Cherokee national treasury would compensate Drew's militia, and Drew was authorized to purchase ammunition and supplies, provided that the expedition was not unnecessarily protracted and did not incur needless expenses.

Ross told Indian Agent Pierce M. Butler about the expedition and asked him to inform the commander at Fort Gibson and the Creek and Choctaw chiefs. The commander at Fort Gibson loaned Drew twenty-five pounds of gunpowder for the militia.

On November 21, Drew left Webbers Falls with eighty-seven well-armed men in his command. By November 26 they had arrived at the site of the battle between the slaves and the Creeks and Cherokees.

Picking up the runaways' trail, Drew's command came upon the bodies of slave hunters Edwards and Wilson, who apparently had been dead about four days. The militia found the trail again and two days later found the fugitives about seven miles north of the Red River, some 280 miles from Fort Gibson.

The slaves offered no resistance; starving, they surrendered immediately. Drew captured thirty-one slaves—the entire group except two who were away hunting. Drew's men returned the slaves to the Cherokee Nation with no problem, arriving at Webbers Falls by December 7.

Drew reported to the Cherokee National Council on December 8. After an investigation, council members ordered five slaves to be held at Fort Gibson pending trial for the murders of Wilson and Edwards, then told Drew to deliver the remaining slaves to their owners. The Choctaw male slave was also turned over to Fort Gibson authorities. Drew kept the two Choctaw slave women and five children in custody until the Cherokees could ascertain their disposition from the Choctaw Nation. Joseph Vann took most of his black rebels out of the Cherokee Nation and put them to work on his steamboat, which worked the Arkansas, Mississippi, and Ohio rivers.

The Cherokees thought the influence of "foreign" free blacks had caused the slave insurrection. On December 2 they passed "An Act in Regard to Free Negroes" directing that all free blacks, except those whom Cherokees had freed, leave the Cherokee Nation by January 1, 1843, or as soon after as possible. Those who lingered or refused would be expelled. The act targeted the free black Seminoles living in the Cherokee Nation.

Cherokee attitudes against free black Seminoles continued. In 1849, tired of harassment from slave-catchers, some of the free black Seminoles under black Chief John Horse fled Indian Territory. They joined Seminole Chief Wild Cat and his followers and successfully reached Mexico.

By 1851, nearly 300 blacks had tried to escape from Indian Territory, most headed for Mexico or Kansas. In the northern Cherokee Nation, in what would later become Washington County, Oklahoma, an "underground railroad" trail led into Kansas. None of the escapes, however, equaled the scope or violence of the Cherokee slave revolt of 1842.

CHAPTER 9

MURRELL HOME

WHAT ABOUT THE SLAVES?

Shirley Pettengill, retired manager of the Murrell Home

First published in the newsletter Friends of Murrell Home 12, no. 2, and will appear in a compilation book edited by Pettengill and Jennifer Sparks to be titled Hunters Home of the Ross and Murrell Families.

A series of exhibit panels located on the second floor at the historic Murrell Home, Oklahoma Historical Society site located at Park Hill, outlines what life was like for slaves prior to the Civil War and touches on some of what was known about the Murrell family's slaves. To understand the history of this historic home, the lives of all of its inhabitants need to be examined. The following article gives some additional information on some of those slaves who were part of "Hunter's Home" plantation in the Cherokee Nation of Indian Territory.

There are a few primary source documents that tell us something about the slaves who lived and worked at the plantation owned by George and Amanda Murrell. The 1860 slave census from Yell County, AR (extending over Indian Territory), indicates that George Murrell owned 42 slaves and that there were nine dwellings for them. The census does not list names or occupations, only their ages and sex. There were 17 males and 25 females. The four oldest males ranged in age from 35–60, seven were 19–28, four were 10–12 and one boy was a year old. Six of the females were 30–35, six were 12–18 and the remaining 12 were less than eight years of age. With 22 of the children below 18, it appears there were likely several families represented.

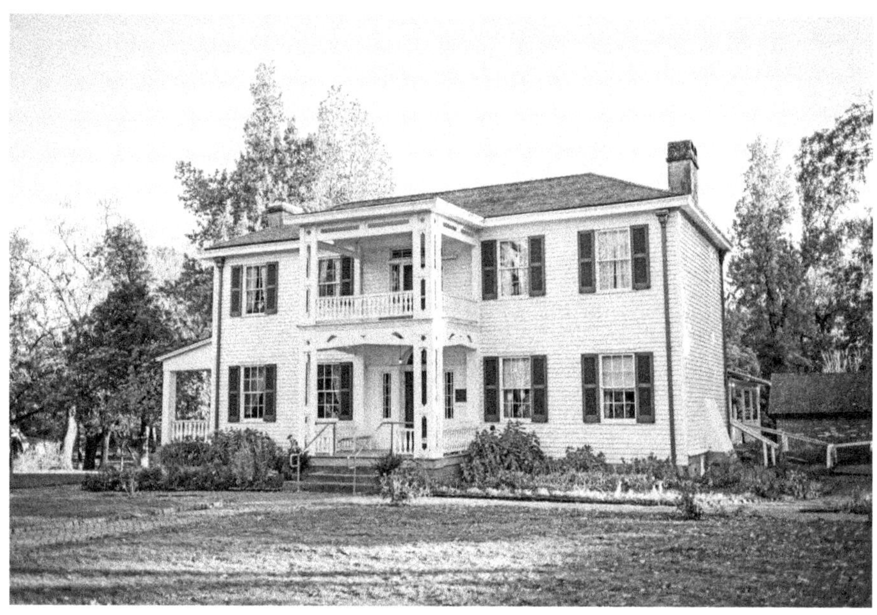

Above: The Murrell Home's mistresses were Cherokee women, and one was credited with saving the home from destruction in the Civil War. *Friends of the Murrell Home.*

Right: Omar Reed, a living history interpreter at Fort Gibson Historical Site, portrays a blacksmith during an event at the antebellum Murrell Home in Park Hill. *George M. Murrell Home Historic Site.*

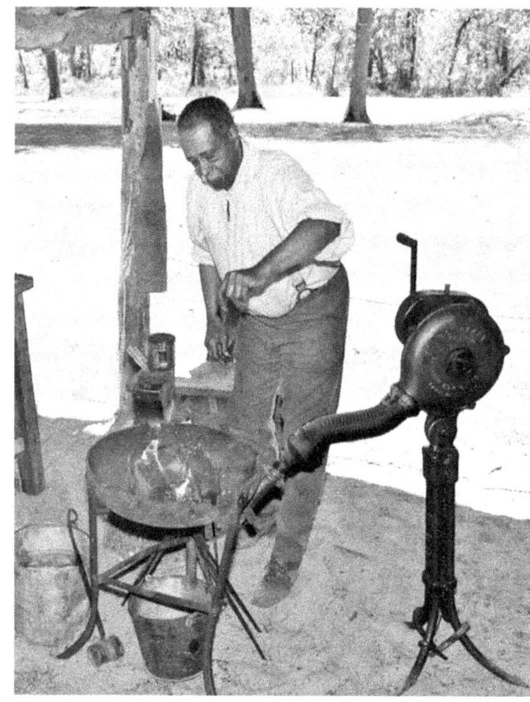

Both George and Amanda (Ross) Murrell, and George's first wife, Minerva (Ross) Murrell, had been raised with the institution of slavery in their prosperous families. George inherited five slaves (Mary and her four children) from his father in 1842. His father's will in Virginia indicated that he had owned 13 slaves at the time of his death. It isn't known if George kept these slaves or perhaps sold them to his siblings or their families back East, as was often the custom.

Probably Minerva, and later Amanda, brought personal servants and perhaps other slaves with them when they married George. The Cherokee census taken in 1835 found that George and Minerva had four slaves. The 1860 census shows that their father, Lewis Ross, owned 51 slaves, more than any other individual in the Cherokee Nation. Besides a plantation, he also ran a saline extracting salt from a brine lake at what is now Salina. His brother, Chief John Ross, is listed as owning 46 slaves. However, many of Amanda's cousins who owned slaves had fewer, usually ranging from five to ten. The majority of Cherokees who did own slaves probably only had one or two. Most Cherokees did not own any slaves, particularly the full bloods who usually practiced subsistence agriculture and did not have the resources to purchase them.

The 1850 slave census in Louisiana indicates that George's brother, John Dobbins, had a sugar plantation and owned 85 slaves. After his brother's death in 1856, George and a nephew acquired this plantation and operated it until shortly before the Civil War when it was sold. The new owner could not pay for it because of the War's devastation, so it was returned to the Murrells and they continued to operate it after the War.

Prior to the Civil War, the Murrells would spend winters in Bayou Goula, Louisiana at "Tally Ho" when the sugar cane was harvested and then return to spend the summers at "Hunter's Home" in the Cherokee Nation. It is likely that some of the same slaves, particularly those designated "house slaves" made the trip with them. Some of them may have also been "family slaves" who came from their original homes in Virginia or Tennessee with the Murrell or Ross family members. After the War, some of the former slaves who were working at the sugar plantation in Louisiana listed their last name as Ross.

No documents have been found regarding the treatment of slaves at Murrell's plantation other than an advertisement in the *Cherokee Advocate* in 1842 regarding a runaway slave named Spencer. It is not known if he was eventually caught or escaped.

Another document that gives a little more information about the Murrell slaves is a diary written by George's niece, Emily Murrell, when she visited her uncle for three months in 1850. Emily brought her personal servant Margaret (inherited from her grandfather) but she mentions four other slaves who were apparently part of Murrell's plantation: Susan, who appears to have been a house servant, Bill, a man or boy who drove a wagon; and Andy and Humphrey, young boys who helped around the house or with the horses.

During a visit to Virginia in the late 1990s, Murrell Home staff found a slave list that is believed to have belonged to George Murrell, as some of the names correlate with those mentioned in Emily's diary. The list appears to have been an inventory of property Murrell lost when the family left Park Hill in 1862 during the Civil War. There were 24 slaves listed as well as equipment and stock. Letters from Ross family members indicate that none of the Murrell slaves had been left at "Hunter's Home" during the period members of the Ross family lived there after 1862.

This list of Murrell's is more extensive, giving names, ages, sometimes occupations, and apparently, family groupings. Eliza, the cook, is 38 with six children listed under her name, ages 2 to 19. Mose is a wagoner {teamster}, his wife Patience is a washer {laundress} and they have four children listed below them, ages 1 to 7. Andy is the waiter, Fayette and Grand are blacksmiths and Tom is a field hand. All are in their late 20s. Nelson, at 40, is the oldest and a boy of 12, Chug, is listed under him. Ike and Peggy, both in their mid-20s, may be a couple. His occupation isn't listed but she was the family's nurse. Susan, at 34, is the family's seamstress and Sylvia, perhaps her 16-year old daughter, is a house servant. Winny, at 26, is the last name on the list.

We believe that when the federal troops came into this area in the summer of 1862, Murrell may have taken some of the other slaves and valuables to Arkansas to prevent their confiscation by the Union. We know Murrell had relatives in Van Buren, and he may have taken his slaves there for safekeeping or have sold them. He may have realized by 1862 that the Ross family might eventually end up supporting the Union. Murrell would never have supported the North but he would never have supported Stand Watie's Confederate troops, as they were enemies of the Ross faction. His only real option once he realized Amanda and their son were safe was to eventually return to Virginia and support the Confederacy from there.

Amanda Murrell was still in Park Hill when many of the Ross men were arrested by the Union troops for signing a Confederate treaty. These men were later pardoned and, along with their families, were escorted to Kansas and eventually made their way to the East as refugees. One source noted there were 16 carriages of the extended Ross families that left with the military entourage.

The slave list found in Virginia may have been the household and other essential slaves left with Amanda while George was in Arkansas. When he was stranded there, the Ross families would never have left Amanda and her infant son at "Hunter's Home" alone in hopes that George Murrell could soon return to Park Hill, so his family also became part of the exodus. Eventually Amanda and her son were able to rejoin her husband in Virginia, probably by passing through the lines under a truce flag.

Many of the slaves who had been left at "Hunter's Home" may well have been part of the entourage that left Park Hill as their servants and were driving the carriages that eventually arrived at Fort Scott in Kansas. It may be that some of them, such as Peggy, the nurse, and Susan, the seamstress, continued on to New York with Amanda. Nothing more is known of them. It is likely that many of the younger men joined the black troops that served in the Kansas Regiments.

Union correspondence near North Fork in the Cherokee Nation in February 1864 stated that "Andy Murrell, the scout, is severely but I think not dangerously wounded." It seems quite likely that this is the Andy mentioned in Emily's diary and on the slave list. After the war an Andy Murrell is listed as having been a resident of Big Sarah Gibson's hotel near Agency Hill in Muskogee. There were no other Murrells besides George's family in the Cherokee Nation. However, there is a family of Creek Freedman after allotment named Murrell. Perhaps Murrell's slave Andy married one of these women. The other young men are even harder to follow. A Lafayette {Fayette?} Merrill served with the 79th U.S. Colored Infantry as did a Dennis Merrill. An Isaac Merrill {Ike?} served with the 83rd Regiment, U.S. Colored Infantry. Lafayette was one of those black soldiers who were massacred after surrendering to Confederates troops at Poison Springs, Arkansas in April 1864. Whether these men were Murrell's former slaves is unknown, but the change in spelling could be attributed to the fact that these men were all probably unable to read and write.

Nelson Murrell, at 40, is the oldest slave on Murrell's list in 1862 and he eventually became the patriarch of the "Freedmen family" that settled in the Snow Creek and Goose Neck Bend area north of Lenapah and south of Coffeyville, Kansas. He stated in his interview that he was "part of the slaves that went out of the Cherokee Nation" with the Ross families when they left and ended up staying in the Fort Scott area. In the 1860s he was driving wagons for someone who was delivering flour to the Osages. That was when they found the land in Goose Neck Bend where a "colony" of former slaves settled.

When he applied for Freedman status with the Dawes Commission in 1901, Nelson said he was 77 years old, that his father was Robert Ross who was owned by Chief John Ross, and his mother was Mariah Nave, who was owned by Susannah (Ross) Nave, sister of Chief John Ross. Nelson's first wife, Eliza Williams, had died by then but he stated that she had been owned by Buffalo Head Williams, who lived about a half-mile to the southwest of the Murrell Home. Nelson and Eliza's daughter, Sarah, had died by 1901 but her husband, Joe Ross, was one of the original settlers in that area. Joe was 70 and was originally owned by Chief John Ross. Joe and Sarah had at least two girls who had died before allotment, but Joe was applying for their sons as well as himself. In the end, a group of at least nine former slaves who had settled in the Snow Creek area near Lenapah, had their claims rejected. The government stated that they didn't arrive until after February 1867, the cut-off date for returning slaves to qualify for becoming Cherokee Freedmen. Nelson and five others in the group are listed as Colored Non-Citizens in the 1870 Census of the Cherokee Nation.

Nelson's second wife, Flora Vann, had been an escaped slave for at least four years before the War started. She lived in a cave, met periodically with her husband and had three children during that period. She never left the Cherokee Nation during or after the War so she was allotted land by the Dawes Commission. She died before the process was completed so her children received her land.

The twelve-year-old boy named Chug who was raised by Nelson Murrell, later used the name of George Henry Murrell. He states his parents were Judy Murrell and Joe Flowers. Their names do not appear on Murrell's list, indicating that they may have been removed from Murrell's plantation before 1862. In 1901, Henry applied for allotment but was found to be living in Kansas, as was his mother Judy and a sister named Lucy Ann. His stepfather, Caesar Murrell, had died near Fort Scott. He also stated that he had a brother named Dennis Murrell who had died in 1875, probably the soldier listed on the 79th Regiment roster.

The last group listed by Murrell was Mose, Patience and their daughters, Lydia, Eliza, Perra and Mary. Years later Eliza and Mary's husband, Moses Lonien, would recount stories of their family's lives during the Civil War in interviews with the WPA. They too had refugeed in Kansas and endured near starvation during summer droughts and severe winters. Eliza noted that her parents actually belonged to Lewis Ross and that her father had taken the last name of Hardrick from a previous owner as there were too many men named Mose Ross. Lydia and Perra apparently did not survive, but by the mid-1870s, four more children had been born. The family settled in the Vinita area and applied for allotment but they were denied as having returned to the Cherokee Nation too late to become citizens. An 1870 census found them in the Delaware District as Colored Non-Citizens.

Reading some of the former slave interviews, it appears that Lewis Ross may have been in the process of giving some of his family's slaves to his children. Mose and his family were with the Murrells, another slave was the cook for daughter Araminta Vann, and two of the cook's children stated they were with William Potter Ross whose wife, Mollie, was another daughter of Lewis Ross.

During our research we were able to locate a descendant of Joe and Sarah (Murrell) Ross in Lenapah. Two descendants of Mose and Patience Hardrick were found living in eastern Oklahoma. In spite of the many difficulties endured by their ancestors during their years of slavery and the Civil War that followed, once they had gained their freedom, some of their descendants were finally able to prosper and became teachers and professional administrators.

CHAPTER 10

ZACHARIAH FOREMAN

"THE WEALTHIEST MAN...IN THE CHEROKEE NATION"

Karen Coody Cooper

Zachariah Foreman, known as Zach or Zack, was a successful merchant, rancher, farmer and founder of the black town of Foreman in the southern Sequoyah District of the Cherokee Nation in 1890. He was born in Indian Territory in the latter 1840s to Jerry and Rhodie Foreman, slaves of Cherokee citizen George Washington Gunter. Gunter was a friend and political colleague of Chief John Ross yet exhibited more sympathy to the Confederacy than had Ross, who was realistically concerned about the perils of abandoning federal treaties.

Zach began life as a slave and by law had received no education and therefore was unable to read or write (his signature was an "X"). However, he was uncannily smart, ambitious and entrepreneurial, coming of age at the end of the Civil War. His father Jerry Foreman's statements recorded by the Dawes Commission in 1901 focus on information regarding his family with a second wife (interviews rarely mentioned offspring already out of the home). Jerry's age was reported as seventy, residing in Sequoyah District and having been a slave of George Gunter, which matches up with son Zach's details. Jerry reported that he had been at Fort Smith on his own during the war before returning to the Cherokee Nation. Zach's interviews, on the other hand, reveal nothing about Civil War experiences when he was a child.

One prophetic day after the Civil War, cattle buyers arrived where Zach was working and purchased a herd of cattle. One of the young cows went lame during the roundup, and the cattle drivers deemed her worthless for their use and let Zach take her. Zach tended to the young cow, and she healed and bore a heifer calf, encouraging Zach to begin accumulating a herd of his own, according to (J.J.) Cape's WPA interview in 1938. After being deemed an approved Cherokee Freedman, Zach could fence unclaimed land within the Cherokee Nation. One could take as much as one could fence and would put to use. Most individuals were happy to claim small plots for farms, but Zach had big dreams. He eventually enclosed three thousand acres of land in the Sequoyah District on the southern end of the Cherokee Nation below Muldrow and above Redland.

Zach was not one to put all his eggs in one basket. Cattle could be stolen, get sick or die, so he also raised cotton and soon built a general store. Realizing that he had created a town, he petitioned for a post office, which opened in 1898. George Washington Gunter had been the first person to establish a cotton gin in the Cherokee Nation in 1844, and his machinery was capable of picking seeds from four to five thousand pounds of cotton daily. Zach likely gained valuable personal experience using Gunter's mechanized gin when laboring for Gunter as a youngster, and Zach constructed his own cotton gin.

Another Freedman interview with the Dawes Commission reveals that Zach had fathered a child named Mattie Foreman in 1880. The girl admitted no memory of ever meeting her father, but witnesses (including a member of the Gunter family) stated in interviews that Zach publicly acknowledged being her father. Young Mattie's mother, Nannie Franklin, sent the child to be raised by an older aunt named Polly Ballard, who lived in the Cooweescoowee District in the north. As an adult, Mattie knew little of her mother, who married three times while remaining in Sequoyah District. This daughter of Zach grew up and married Jackson Vann and had three children: Eli, Ora and Jennie Vann. The Vann family lived in Wagoner, and her Freedmen files are found under the name of Maggie Vann.

Zach eventually married Mattie Bell, who had been born in Texas in 1864 and taught at a Negro school before they married sometime after 1880. She became the postmistress of Foreman, and they started a family that grew to six children who survived childhood: Edgar (October 29, 1885–April 26, 1967), Sheridan (born circa 1886), Roscoe Wallace (May 1890–December 1941), Zack Jr. (July 1893–September 1921), Urah/Rhoda B. (born circa 1894) and Odis Dewey Foreman (born December 15, 1898).

Zach and Mattie were determined to provide a strong education for their children. The Julius Rosenwald Fund, a nationwide effort to improve educational services for underserved blacks in the southern states, helped fund a public school through junior high level in Foreman, including a vocational training room and living quarters for single teachers. The school had its own light plant and was situated on ten acres of Needmore Hill, where training in agriculture could also occur. The town of Foreman grew to support three churches, a Masonic lodge and a few businesses.

When the Missouri Pacific Railroad/Kansas City Southern line bypassed Foreman, Zach apprised railroad officials of how much business he could provide, and they agreed to lay rails if he first prepared a suitable railroad bed. Those who owed him debts were welcome to work off their debts by laboring on the project, plus those who needed work, or extra work, were hired. Soon the spur was laid and operating.

J.J. Cape's 1938 Indian-Pioneer Papers interview detailed incidents citing the generosity and sensitivity of Zach, who had aided Cape's family when Cape's mother became ill, needing specialized medical care. Even though Cape's father was a doctor, the family could not afford to obtain the treatments the mother needed, and when Zach heard about their troubles, he loaned the family the needed money. One day, Cape's father was taking cotton to the Foreman gin when a heavy rain began. Zach invited Cape's father to stay at his home and had a table set for him for dining, and the doctor/farmer was "taken to a room to sleep where no colored people ever slept. This was reserved for white people." Zach knew perfectly well how to advantageously navigate the world he had created in Foreman.

Zach and Mattie held an annual Emancipation Proclamation Picnic every August 4, providing a barbecue, games and dancing. He and his wife were always crowned king and queen of the festival and rode a pair of black horses while passing in review before the crowning ceremony. Cape reported that the wealthy couple was beloved by all.

But life would not proceed as a continuously happy party. Historian William T. Hagan reported that during the 1891 election campaigns in the Cherokee Nation, someone raised the issue about "old Zach Foreman, near Webbers Falls [having] colonized nearly one hundred worthless Alabama negroes" to cultivate "several thousand acres of the best agricultural lands in the Cherokee nation." When someone succeeds, there is always jealousy voiced furiously with bias, especially during political campaigns.

For Zach, emotionally painful years now lay ahead. Mattie died in 1900, at the age of thirty-six, and is buried at Center Point Cemetery in Redland alongside the graves of the couple's four lost infants. Richard Foreman, Zach's half brother, became the postmaster in 1900, serving through 1904.

In December 1902, the *Stilwell Standard* reported that "the fine home of Zack Foreman, the richest Cherokee freedman in the nation, was burned last week. Richard Foreman's son (probably Benjamin) and Sapulpa Wear, two colored people were burned to death in the fire." Richard Foreman (born in October 1852) and son Benjamin (born in 1880) are buried at Center Point Cemetery, as are Zach's son Ed and his wife, along with Zach Sr., Zach Jr., Roscoe and Urah B. (who married Mr. W.A. Rowell in 1920). Sheridan and Odis Dewey are either buried elsewhere or were buried at Center Point without headstones (or the stones disappeared at some time).

In 1904, commissioners of the Cherokee Land Office interviewed Zach (mistakenly recorded as Jack), noting in 1902 that he possessed sections noted as E2, SE4, NW4 and Lots 6 and 7 of "Section 3, T. 9 N., R. 25 E." that were not yet filed on. It seems that he was to sell any improvements directly to claimants desiring those lands, and he reported that he had done so in some cases, while in other cases people changed their mind. He had to clarify for the commissioners the lands he'd sold before the Dawes Allotment Act went into effect, which lands were in process of being claimed by others and which parcels remained to be allotted. His answers are patient, succinct and clear. He cited the pending disposition of nine full allotments from his land. He reported which eighty acres he had filed on, retaining his home and other houses and fencing near the Antioch Church. Reading the typewritten interview, it seemed that Zach was more self-assured, knowledgeable, patient and professional than the interviewer. The 1904 interview reveals a man, at the age of fifty-five, still at the top of his mental abilities.

The act of allotment of the communal lands of the Cherokee Nation dramatically reduced Zach's landholdings, diminishing his ability to continue his income-producing operations as before. He was denied the opportunity to leave wealth to his children, and his legacy was undermined. The breaking up of his holdings called for effort on his part, as he aided others in initiating claims on his parcels, perhaps with the purpose of ensuring that his neighbors were practically hand-selected and would be people he knew and trusted. The fate of the cotton gin is not known, and he likely managed to retain ownership of it, if it was still lucrative.

Angie Debo documented the abuse of allottees in her seminal book *And Still the Waters Run*. The allotments went into effect in 1908, starting what Debo termed an "orgy of buying land from allottees" who were often more desperate for money than land. She noted that one commissioner made "an especially earnest attempt to call attention to the exploitation of Five Tribes allottees [visiting] twenty or thirty Negro cabins on the rich land around

Muskogee about 1913. He found only two persons of the group who had retained their land."

In 1910, a badly spelled federal census list of the Foreman family cites names as Zachari, Sherdan, Rosco W., Zachoria R. Jr., Rhoda B. and Odis D. living in one household in Redland. Before discovering this record, I had been unable to locate Dewey in his adult years, having never before seen him referred to as Odis.

In January 1911, a Zach Foreman was charged with robbing the Foreman Post Office. Was this the elder or younger Zach, or perhaps a third Zach who lived in the region? In any case, the accused was acquitted by a jury trial in Sequoyah County, according to the January 1911 *Muskogee Times-Democrat*. Perhaps it had been a bookkeeping error or an error in judgment rather than out-and-out theft.

Zach died on August 5, 1916, at about sixty-seven years of age. His funeral was attended by all walks of life, by blacks, whites and Indians, reported the *Fort Gibson New Era*. He had been hailed in 1891 by the *Indianapolis Freeman* as "the wealthiest man, white or black, in the Cherokee Nation." While that honorific failed to include a comparison with wealthy Indians, the achievements of Zach were indeed noteworthy. He was also declared to be "the only Negro in the United States at that time who privately owned a railroad." While he owned not a railroad business but rather a spur of tracks, that accomplishment also remains a heady achievement.

Angie Debo reported that six Muskogee attorneys were investigated with regard to the guardianships of wealthy Negro minors wherein guardians had extracted exorbitant fees while serving their appointments. One judge noted regarding the suit of a "young freedman [who] was fighting to secure possession of his property" that Muskogee had probably lost one hundred wealthy allottees who would have productively stayed in Muskogee had they dared, but due to the detrimental treatment they'd received, most had left the area entirely. Allotment certainly served to reduce the success and power of the Cherokee Nation by diverting Cherokee accomplishments in nation building, including schools and government buildings, to white control.

The *Muldrow Sun* reported on February 27, 1920, that Roscoe had been named administrator of Zach's estate and that the heirs were established as Ed, Sheridan, Roscoe, Zach Jr., Dewey and Rhoda (Urah), all being noted as issue of the deceased. The Foreman offspring would share in an estate valued at just over $10,000, a nice sum of money in 1920, but less than Zach's previous riches—it was too little to provide his children and grandchildren with the comforts they had experienced earlier in life.

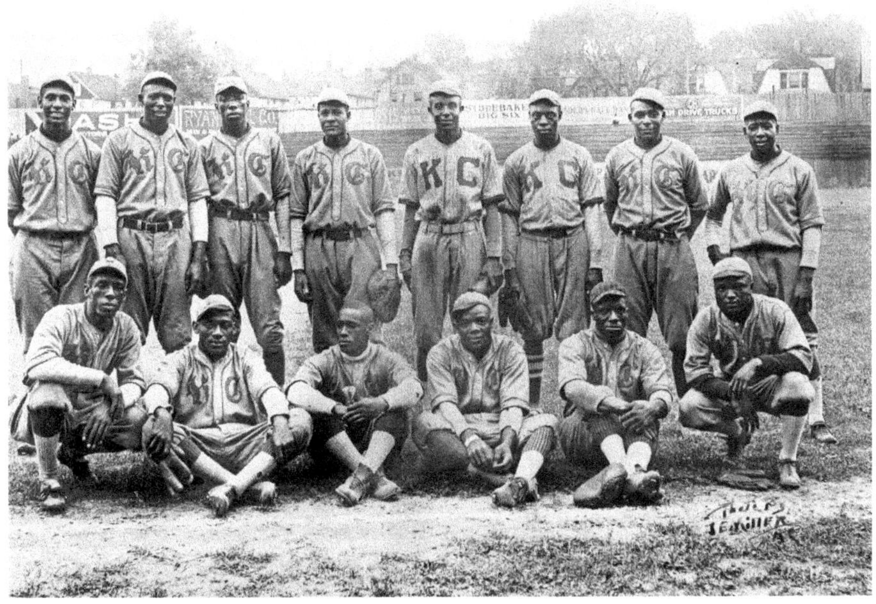

Zach Foreman Jr. (*standing, fourth from right*) played professional baseball with the Negro National League's Kansas City Monarchs in 1919–20 before his untimely death. *National Baseball Hall of Fame and Museum.*

The upward and downward spirals of the Foreman family continued in the children's lives. Son Zachariah Foreman Jr., born in July 1893, entered a life far different from that experienced by his parents during their childhoods. Zach Jr. attended the colored school at Langston and went on to become a professional baseball player in 1920, serving as his team's pitcher for a few years. He was joined in that endeavor in 1921 by cousin Sylvester Foreman (son of Benjamin), who signed up as the catcher for the Negro National League's Kansas City Monarchs, according to Ashwill's "Not All Ball Players Are Broke." Sylvester, known as "Hooks," played ball for a dozen years, appearing with various teams. He died in 1940 and is buried in Coffeyville, Kansas, near the Oklahoma border.

Zach Jr. is touted as having purchased a very expensive vehicle, a Locomobile Model 48, introduced in 1919 for the astonishing price of $10,000. It was a handsome oversized limousine convertible, and obviously young Zach had managed to expend more money than his baseball employment would have provided. He seemed to be maintaining the glory days his father had initiated and possibly was doing so on a good line of credit. He might have expected to inherit more than he actually did at the final disbursement of his father's estate.

During a visit home in 1921, young Zach was participating in a poker game in Foreman when an argument erupted. He drew his gun, driving the troublemaker to leave the premises. Later, when Zach Jr. left the building, he was shot in the back of the head and died at the age of twenty-seven near the cotton gin his father had built. His assailant was prosecuted and served time, but the Foreman siblings were probably left reeling from the loss.

But the rest of the family carried on. Eldest son Ed married Peggy Plunkett and raised three daughters: Edna M., Thelma S. and Juanita. They lived in Redland in 1930.

Second son Sheridan Foreman is found on the 1930 census in Redland, widowed and boarding on a farmstead. In 1920, he was living in the household of Sallie Foreman, widow of his older relative Richard, perhaps an uncle. No children are apparent for Sheridan. He is noted as having served in World War I. He does not appear to have been wealthy.

Son Roscoe is known to have attended the Colored High School, graduating in 1908. He signed up for the draft and later became the Foreman postmaster in 1930, and he is found on the census that year boarding with a local family. The Depression and Dust Bowl soon decimated the area economy to its lowest, and the Foreman Post Office closed in 1936, leaving the town to fade away to almost invisible ruins. Roscoe married Luella Williams in 1938 and took up residence in Muldrow. His records show no sign of children or wealth.

Urah B., the surviving daughter, was living in 1920 with three of her siblings (excepting Sheridan and Ed). The four offspring resided together on Foreman Street in Redland. She married later that year, but her husband, W.A. Rowell, is noted as widowed on the 1930 census and married again in 1938. He was a mortician at Fort Smith, Arkansas. It does not appear that Urah had children.

Youngest son Odis Dewey was born on December 15, 1899, and registered for the draft in 1918. He was married by 1924 when the couple was sued for $1,926 they owed on a loan, according to the November 7, 1924 *Democrat-American*. It seems Dewey had no wealth, and it is not known if he had offspring.

While the patriarch's economic accomplishments were amazing at the time, Oklahoma statehood and allotment served to diminish Zachariah Foreman's legacy. Compounding the hardship of lost land were the Dustbowl and the Great Depression, as well as repressive racism and KKK activities in the area. Had things been different, the town of Foreman might have thrived, and Zach's ranch might have continued as a family stronghold. Zach set a magnificent example of ambition and financial success that few others could emulate in northeastern Oklahoma for generations to follow.

References

Ancestry.com, including access to census and family records; Find-A-Grave cemetery pages; Fold 3 documents of Freedmen interviews; Dawes applications; military records and so on.

Ashwill, Gary. "Not All Ball Players Are Broke: Zack Foreman of the Kansas City Monarchs." *Agate Type*, blog, September 25, 2011.

Ballenger, T.L. "The Colored High School of the Cherokee Nation." *Chronicles of Oklahoma* 30, no. 4 (1952).

Canada, J. Craig. "If the Legends Are True." Found at palmspringsalbum.org/genealogy/getperson.php?personID=145690&tree=Legends.

Cape, J.J. WPA interview. Indian-Pioneer Papers, Oklahoma Historical Society, 1938.

Debo, Angie. *And Still the Waters Run: The Betrayal of the Five Civilized Tribes.* Princeton, NJ: Princeton University Press, 1940. Reprinted by University of Oklahoma Press, 1989.

Hagan, William T. *Taking Indian Lands.* Norman: University of Oklahoma Press, 2003.

Indianapolis Freeman. November 28, 1891.

Miller, Melinda C. *The One Thing Needful: Land and Black Mobility, 1880 to 1900.* N.p., n.d.

Muskogee-Times Democrat. January 1911, 8.

Oklahoma History Center, East Indian Territory. Oklahoma Historical Society, Oklahoma City, Oklahoma. www.okhistory.org/history/blacktowns/town-detail-other.php?Town=19.

Perdue, Theda. *Slavery and the Evolution of Cherokee Society, 1540–1866.* N.p., n.d.

Wikipedia. "Hooks Foreman." https://en.wikipedia.org/wiki/Hooks_Foreman.

CHAPTER 11

BLACK MEMBERS OF THE CHEROKEE NATIONAL COUNCIL

Karen Coody Cooper

In the decades before Oklahoma statehood (and the subsequent closing of Cherokee government), at least six Freedmen were elected to serve on the Cherokee National Council. This information might not have been evident to today's researchers had Cherokee historian and genealogist Emmet Starr not added the notation "the latter a Negro" after each of the names of the six men in the published listing of Cherokee Council members in his 1921 book *History of the Cherokee Indians and Their Legends and Folk Lore.*

From Starr we learn that in 1875 Joseph Brown was elected as a councilman from Tahlequah District; Frank Vann was elected in 1887 representing Illinois District; Jerry Alberty was voted in from Cooweescoowee District in 1889; in 1893, Joseph "Stick" Ross represented Tahlequah District; and in 1895, Samuel Stidham represented Illinois District, while Ned Irons was selected from Tahlequah District.

These men would have received substantial support from various Cherokee voters. They would have been affable gentlemen, demonstrating intelligence, and viewed as admired examples of hardworking family men. The following information has been gleaned from Freedmen rolls and application interviews, cemetery information, census records, published details and the WPA interviews recorded in the 1930s.

JOSEPH BROWN was thirty-two when he was interviewed for enrollment as a Freedman in 1901, making his birth circa 1870. Because his name was quickly verified on earlier rosters, his Dawes interview was short, so we learn little about his life. He was living in Vian, Illinois District, son of Jack/Jacob and Katie Brown, and married to Lula/Lulu Freeman of Conway, Arkansas. They had two children, Dee/Steve and Milton/Melton Brown, and in 1902 added son Joseph Jr. Each birth was certified by a different midwife, which might mean that he and his wife had lived elsewhere earlier. Census records of 1910 (as well as 1920) report the family absent of Joe Jr., which likely means the boy had died. Added to the family were Luther and Viola. Joseph himself was noted on the census as having been born in Alabama, and the family was farming in Sadie, Oklahoma.

FRANK VANN reported in his enrollment interview that he was forty-five or fifty in 1901 and lived in Fort Gibson of Illinois District. His parents were Caleb and Mariah Vann, and his children were Beulah, Lonnie/Larney and Jesse. Frank reported that he had been the slave of John Vann and lived in Webbers Falls before the war, staying at Fort Scott, Kansas, from 1862 through 1866. He did not appear on the 1880 census, leading to a more in-depth interrogation regarding verification of dates and residency. He reported that he met his wife, Julia, while attending school in Tennessee in the 1880s, and they married there, where their older children were born. The fact of him attending school possibly surprised the interviewer. When the interviewer suggested some possible witnesses who might testify regarding Frank's having returned to the Nation after the war, Judge Schrimsher was mentioned, and Frank stated, "I know we were in office together at Tahlequah." The interview stopped, and when the interview resumed, Frank was asked, "Did you ever hold any position in the Cherokee Nation?" and "What was that?" and "When were you elected member of the Council, do you remember?" The interviewer would have been even more overwhelmed had he known more about Frank's father, who had come straight from Africa into Cherokee slavery and led a Cherokee slave rebellion in 1842.

Frank Vann's sister, Betty Robertson, was interviewed in 1937 during the WPA Indian-Pioneer Papers project. She reported that their father, Caleb/Kalet, was one of the leaders of the Cherokee slave revolt. She reported her mother to be Sally and noted her brothers to be Sone/Sonny and Frank, while her sisters were Polly, Ruth and Liddle. She said that many of the slaves employed on Joe Vann's steamboat, *Lucy Walker*, were made to reside and work on the boat away from their families as punishment for their role in the revolt. The ship's boilers exploded during a final fateful trip, killing Caleb and his master along with most of the crew and several passengers. Some

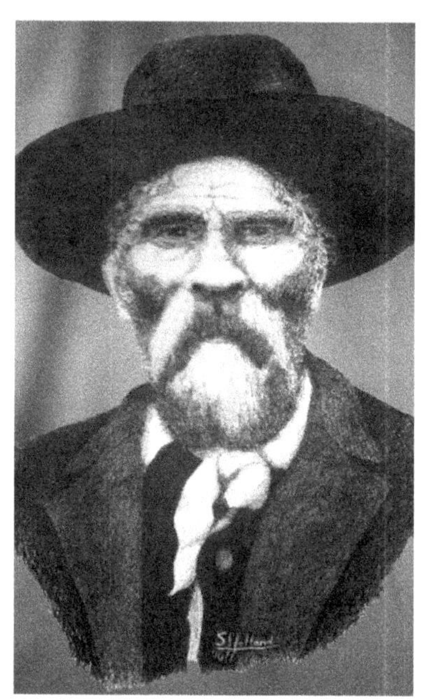

accounts blame Joe Vann for demanding the boiler be stoked for a riverboat race, while others suggested that the disaffected slaves had plotted the explosion.

Frank Vann went on to become an educated man and served as a preacher for the Fort Gibson Colored Baptist Church in 1893 and again in 1901. He might have been an itinerant preacher, a layman who stepped in when a preacher was absent, or he may have been the preacher at the church for an extended time. He and his family are found on the 1900 census. Frank died on July 27, 1909, and Julia died on October 20, 1946; both are buried at Citizens Cemetery at Fort Gibson. Frank's cemetery marker is a

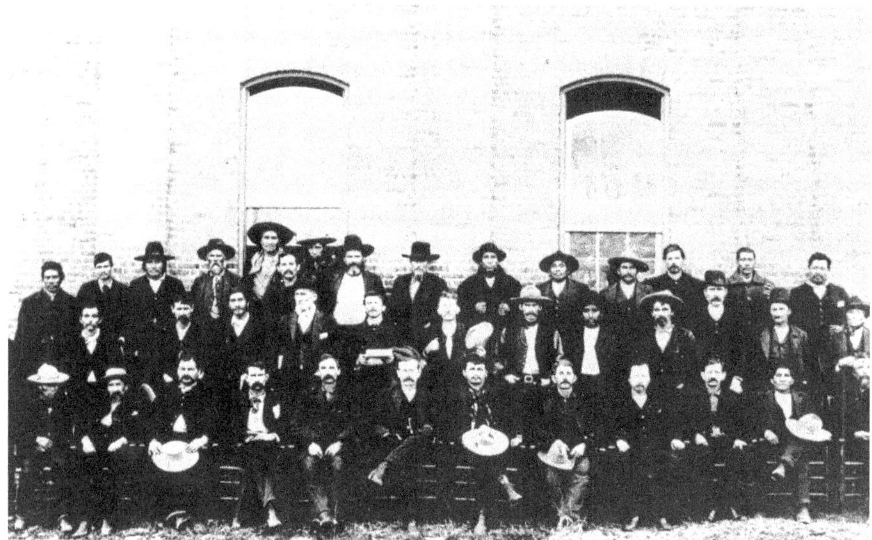

Above: Members of the Council (Lower House) of the National Council of the Cherokee Nation, Tahlequah, 1889 and 1890. Image includes Jerry Alberty (*back row, fourth from the left*). *Western History Collections, University of Oklahoma Library.*

Top: Jerry Alberty was one of six black Cherokee Nation council members serving between the end of the Civil War and statehood. *Sandy Holland.*

white marble spire and reads, "Reverend Frank Vann." Julia died at age ninety-seven according to the hand-inscribed headstone in the cemetery. She lived as a widow for thirty-seven years. In 1920, Julia was living in Nowata as head of household, and her sons Lonnie and Jessie, mature men, resided with her.

JERRY ALBERTY was born in Georgia and died on January 8, 1904, at about the age of seventy, and his grave marker is found among those of other family members at the Jerry Alberty Family Cemetery near Chouteau in Wagoner County. White man Moses Alberty, married to a Cherokee woman and serving as a judge in the Cherokee Nation, sired Jerry, whose mother was slave Sarah. Jerry then became the property of his own half brother, William Alberty.

During the Civil War, the Alberty family (black, white and Cherokee) took refuge in the Choctaw Nation and then the Red River area. Jerry married Ruth West-Marcum, a Cherokee freedwoman, while in Texas, and upon the war's end, they settled in Wagoner. She lived at least eighty-six years. Their children were Louisa (married White), Noah, Moses, Carrie, Joshua, Emory, Sarah, Annie Amelia, Bertha and Hattie. Son Moses named a daughter Ruth after his mother.

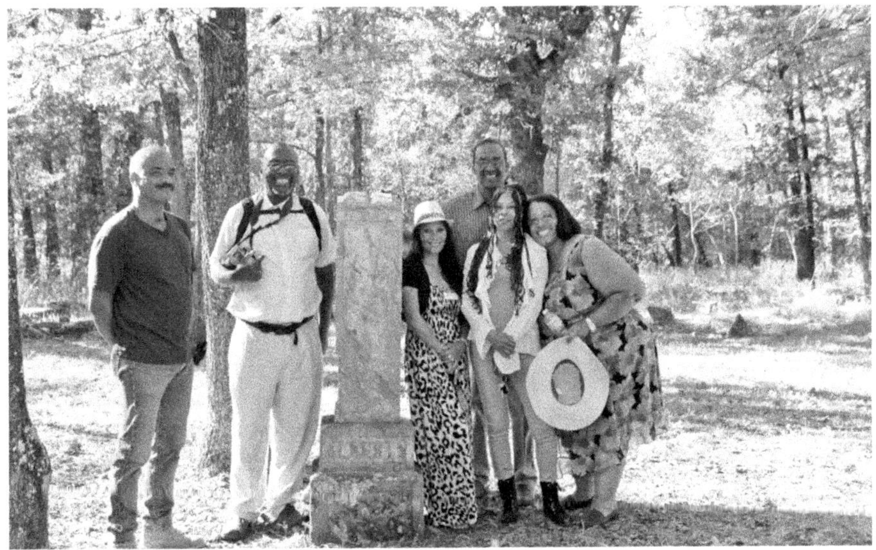

Family and friends surround Jerry Alberty's headstone. *Left to right*: Tony Hubbard, Jeffrey Williams, Heidi Harrison, Rodslen King-Brown and Cindy Williams, with Mark A. Harrison in the back. *Jim Campbell.*

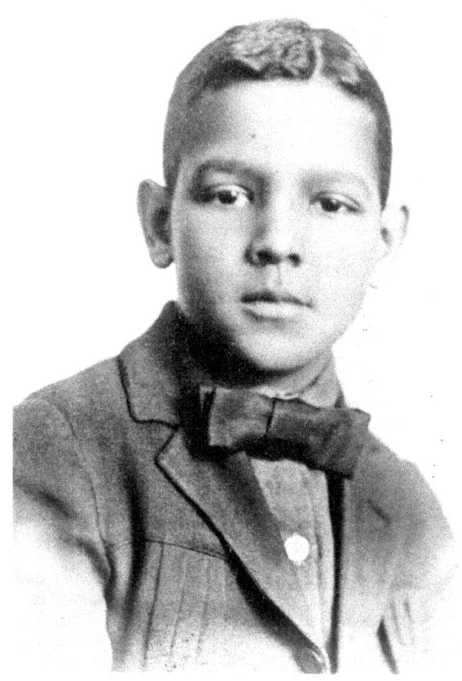

Left: Clem Nave/Alberty observed grandfather Jerry Alberty's life and shared memories with his own grandson Mark A. Harrison. *Mark A. Harrison.*

Below: The Cherokee Nation's capitol building was completed in 1869 utilizing the labor of Stick Ross, who later served as a council member of the Cherokee government. *Jim Roaix.*

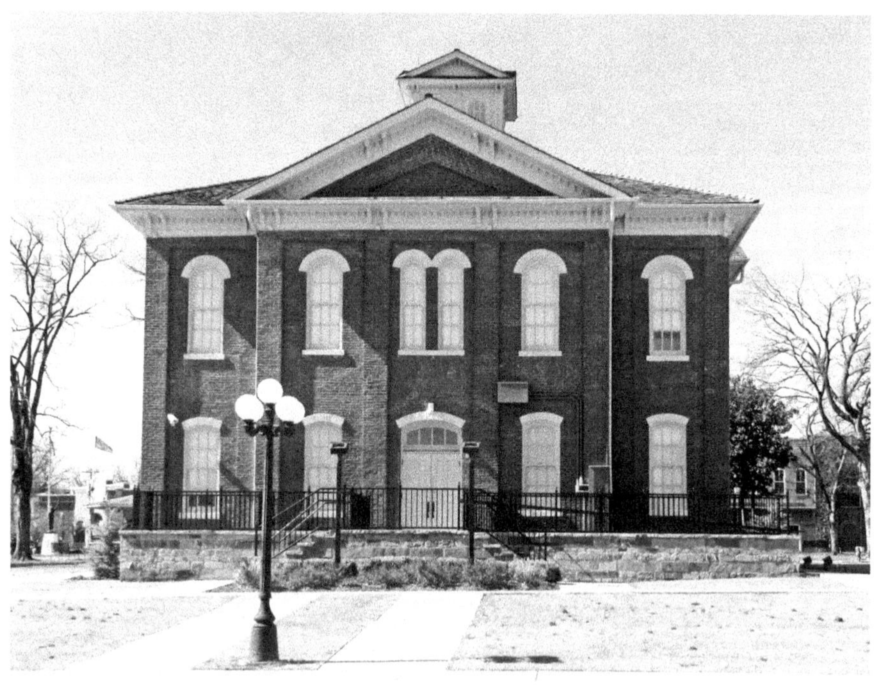

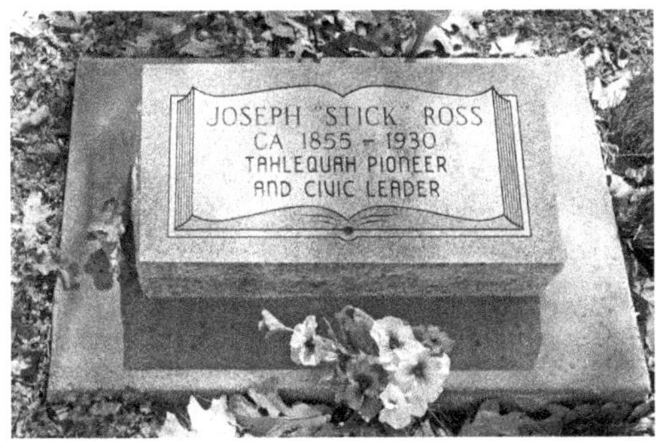

Stick Ross is buried in the cemetery he obtained to protect slave burials, continuing its use as a cemetery during segregation. *Jim Roaix.*

The *Cherokee Advocate* noted on August 14, 1889, "Jerry Alberty, the Colored candidate who ran on the Downing Ticket for Council in Cooweescoowee District, was elected by over one hundred majority, he having received the same support that the rest of the ticket did." Another newspaper account described Alberty as co-hosting a Grand Fishing party at Flat Rock in conjunction with the Sunday church meeting. And in another story, he is noted to have brought a few students for admittance to the Colored School at Double Springs. He is buried at the Jerry Alberty Family Cemetery in Wagoner County. His son Noah married the daughter of another council member, Samuel Stidham. Wife Ruth and son Moses are buried at Sanders Cemetery in Nowata County.

Joseph "Stick" Ross is probably the most publicly familiar of the six council members because Stick Ross Mountain Road preserves his name in the area where he lived after emancipation. He had been a slave of Chief John Ross, and his parents were Hector and Sallie Ross. He was residing in the Saline District in 1880 but was in the Tahlequah District in 1900. Born circa 1850, he first married Margaret Pack, fathering Carrie and Austin. His second wife was Nancy Rowe, and their children were Malcolm, Julia, Amanda, Patsy and Clem. Julie married Lee Funkhouser in 1904, and she and their children are found living with her parents in 1910. That census states that Stick Ross and family were living in Park Hill, farming on their own farm. In 1930, Stick/Steck was recorded as eighty-one years old, and Nancy was said to be seventy-three. Clem, at age thirty, was then living with his parents.

Stick Ross was known to have carried countless hods of mortar during masonry work on the Cherokee National Capitol Building in 1867. He is buried at Ross Cemetery on Bliss Avenue in Tahlequah on land he obtained and donated for the existing cemetery (it had been a slave cemetery, and he wanted to preserve it). His own grave is among the lost sites in the cemetery, as headstones disappeared through vandalism. A monument was placed at the cemetery for Stick Ross in 2008.

Little is known of SAMUEL STIDHAM. His surname was challenging to spell for those recording information, and handwriting of the time was often inaccurately transcribed, plus there was a Creek Freedman named Sam Stidham, easily confused with a Cherokee Freedman of the same name. Samuel Stidham was about forty-five years old in 1901 and living in Fort Gibson when he enrolled himself and his nineteen-year-old daughter, Mary, as Cherokee Freedmen. He noted his parents to be Buck Stidmon and Mary Walker. Sam had a daughter with Sallie McConnell, named Lizzie Stidman, found on the 1900 U.S. census. His wife had been Dollie Taylor, deceased at the time of his interview with the Dawes office. On June 12, 1901, daughter Mary married Noah Alberty, son of Jerry Alberty. Living in Wagoner, they later registered their children, Theodore and Lillian, born in 1905 and 1906.

In 1910, a Sam Stidmon is found living with another wife, Sallie, age forty-two, in Muskogee. Living near him is a likely son, Charley Stidman, thirty-one, with wife Daisy, thirty, and Sammie, four (a likely namesake). In 1920, Samuel is widowed and working as a school janitor, and his neighbor is again Charles, forty-one, with Daisy, thirty-nine, and Ollie G. Stidman (probably Sammie), age fourteen.

NED IRONS was forty-four in 1901, and his wife, Julia, was thirty-eight. Ned's mother was Margaret Bird (her parents were Nero Irons and Fannie Irons Miller, and her siblings were Mollie Nero Johnson and Richard Nero, all of whom signed up as Creek Freedmen). Ned did not report who his father was (and perhaps did not know). His owner had been Anna Rogers Irons. Ned's children were Alice (married Andy Beam), Emma, Polly, Jeff, Henderson (Derson) and Willard.

It is gratifying to follow Ned Irons on the U.S. census all the way through 1930. His marriage to Julia was long and enduring. His children's homes were nestled around their residence. In the 1920 census, son Jeff and his wife live on one side of Ned and Julia's home, while Henderson and his wife live on the other. For someone who never had a chance to know his father, Ned proved to be a successful family man.

The six men ran for office, were elected and served. They were black in a world dominated by red and white. They were the first generation of Freedmen who were allowed to pursue reading and writing and to have their children accepted into classrooms. They could own land, they had the right to keep their familial relationships intact and they could vote and participate in government functions. But the first blush of freedoms would start to recede as the Cherokee Nation lost its right to self-govern, treaty rights dissolved and poverty increased in the area.

References

Cherokee Freedman interviews and census reports. Accessed on Fold 3 at ancestry.com; other genealogical sources also aided in research, including Find-a-Grave.

Miles, Tiya. *The House on Diamond Hill: A Cherokee Plantation Story.* Chapel Hill: University of North Carolina Press, 2010.

Newton, Josh. "Monument to History." *Tahlequah Daily Press*, May 20, 2008.

Robertson, Betty. Interview of 1937. Indian-Pioneer Papers. Oklahoma Historical Society, Oklahoma City.

Starr, Emmet. *History of the Cherokee Indians and Their Legends and Folk Lore.* Reprint, 1921. Originally published, Oklahoma City, OK: Warden Company. Available from Pubmix.com.

West, C.W. "Dub." *Fort Gibson: Gateway to the West.* Muskogee, OK: Muskogee Publishing Company, 1974.

CHAPTER 12

OUTLAW CHEROKEE BILL VERSUS LAWMAN IKE ROGERS

Karen Coody Cooper

The most notorious black Cherokee outlaw, Crawford Goldsby, known as Cherokee Bill, was born in 1876 and executed in Fort Smith, Arkansas, in 1896 when he was only twenty years old. He had killed a number of people during robberies and had grown up fast in a world accelerated by violence. Isaac/Ike Rogers, another black Cherokee, was born circa 1850 and became a deputy U.S. marshal. The lives of Cherokee Bill and Ike Rogers fatefully intertwined. They knew each other socially, but their relationship had been a wary one.

William Lee Starr provided a 1937 WPA interview noting that he had attended a Fort Gibson school with Cherokee Bill in 1882:

> *Goldsby was very apt and good natured as he grew up.... He committed his first crime in the year 1892 or 1893, shooting Jake Lewis, a Freedman. Lewis had seemed to impose upon Clarence, Goldsby's brother, at a dance.... My wife and I were living at Tahlequah in the latter part of 1893 and Goldsby came to his cousin's one night. My wife and I tried to get him to surrender, for both he and Jake Lewis were Freedmen and they would have been tried under the jurisdiction of the Cherokee laws. In a case of that kind, perhaps, he would not have gotten more than six or eight months in prison at Tahlequah. Goldsby said, "No!" He knew nearly every pig trail of the Indian Territory and Mexico. He could burst a squirrel eye, as far*

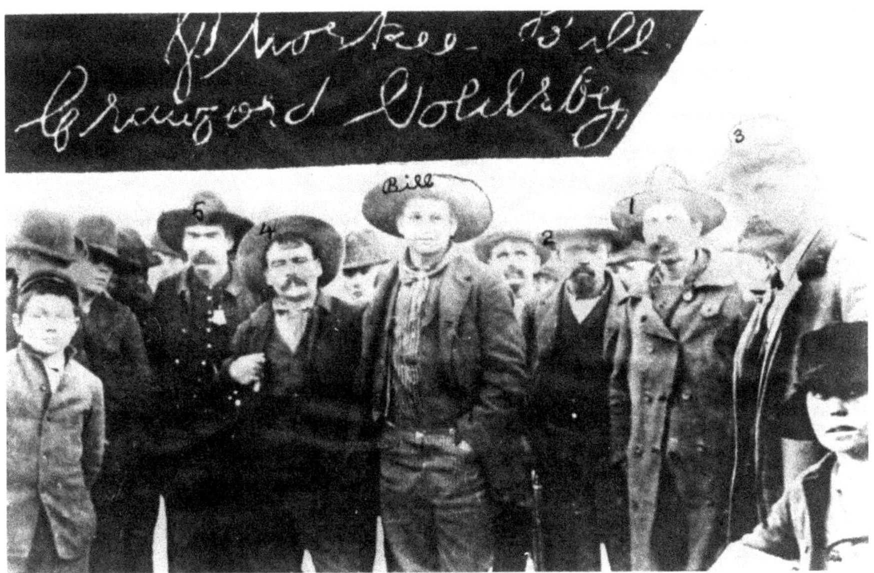

Outlaw Cherokee Bill is shown following his capture by Ike Rogers (no. 2), accompanied by fellow lawmen. *Tulsa Historical Society.*

as he could see, every shot, and he said he could shoot from his waist on a level and hardly ever miss his target.

He took a liking to the stepdaughter of Ike Rogers, a Deputy United States Marshal, and one morning Ike persuaded the girl to get some chickens for breakfast, knowing they would try to see her, and there they trapped him. Ike, with the aid of a man named Clint Scales, overpowered Goldsby and placed him in prison at Fort Smith, after which Clarence Goldsby, Cherokee Bill's brother, never had any more good feeling for Ike.

I was at the Cherokee Freedman payment at Hayden. On one of the dancing platforms Clarence and Ike began a dispute about something concerning the arrest of Cherokee Bill. Ike gave Clarence a shove and made some threat. The officials of the payment decided to move the payment to Fort Gibson. Clarence told Ike Rogers that if he put his foot on the soil of Fort Gibson he would be a dead man.

But Ike was not to be bluffed. He notified Clarence that he would be down on the morning train which arrived in Fort Gibson about 10:30 A.M. and that he was ready for him. I was in Fort Gibson when the payment was going on. Clarence had on the hat of my wife's nephew, Will Pack. Clarence went to a room and put on his six-shooter just a few minutes

> *before the train was due. My wife asked him what he was going to do with that gun and he smiled and said, "Nothing." She said to him, "You had better leave it off," but he went straight to the depot. When the train pulled in and Rogers dismounted, having his face toward the train, Clarence shot him through the neck from behind.*
>
> *After Ike fell on his back, Clarence shot him twice in the face and reached and got Cherokee Bill's gun that Ike had, then passed under a boxcar going east. Some officers began shooting and Clarence returned the fire, and a stray bullet struck T.J. Elliot, one founder of the Elliot firm of Muskogee. Clarence's mother lived one block east of the Missouri Pacific Depot at that time; and a bullet fired by the officers passed through an old buggy as Clarence went through his mother's lot.*

Q.B. Boydstun, author of *Growing Up with Oklahoma*, mentions Cherokee Bill's mother, born as Ellen Beck, half Negro, one quarter Cherokee and one quarter white:

> *One of my clients was a black woman, Aunt Ellen Lynch. A Cherokee Freedman, she was the mother of Crawford Goldsby, also known as "Cherokee Bill," a notorious outlaw hanged by order of Judge Isaac Parker at Fort Smith. I represented her in her effort to obtain a widow's pension as the widow of William Lynch, her second husband, a Civil War soldier. Her first husband was George Goldsby…when he was serving at Fort Gibson with the 10th U.S. Cavalry (Buffalo Soldiers) in the 1870s. She left Fort Gibson when the cavalry was transferred to Fort Bliss, Texas. She had three or four children by Goldsby. Goldsby deserted at Fort Bliss, Texas, and joined up with* [Pancho] *Villa, the Mexican revolutionary.*
>
> *She told me that she went to Fort Smith to see* [her son] *hanged, and she was permitted to see and talk to him before the execution. She stated that the rules would not allow her to witness the execution unless he gave permission. When she promised not to cry, he gave his permission for her to attend. She later said that she kept her promise. After the execution she brought his body back to Fort Gibson, and the funeral was held in her home, at one time the old Fort Chapel.*

A lot happened between the time of Cherokee Bill's first shooting and his hanging. One of the best chronicles of the events is *Marauders of the Indian Nations: The Bill Cook Gang and Cherokee Bill*, written by Glenn Shirley. Cherokee Bill linked up with Jim and Bill Cook in June 1894 when they

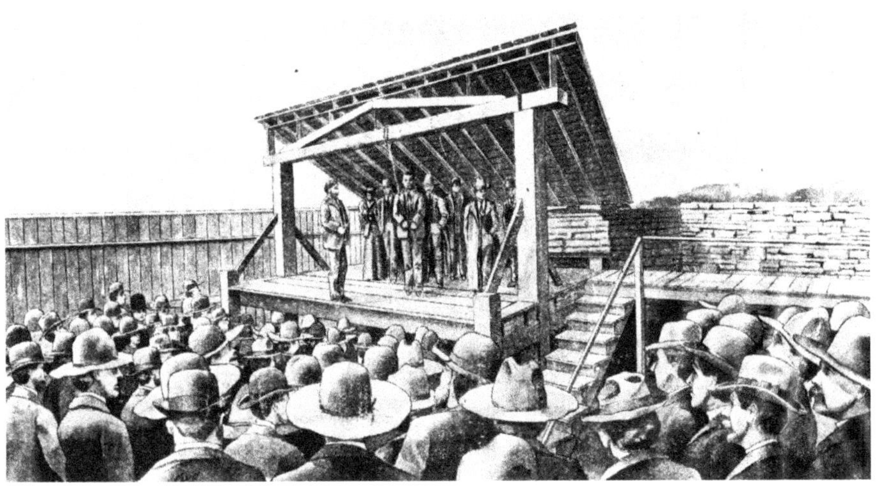

A large crowd attended the hanging of killer Cherokee Bill at the Fort Smith, Arkansas gallows in 1896. *Fort Smith National Historic Site.*

were all involved in a shootout that killed Sequoyah Houston, a Cherokee lawman. After that, the Cook Gang grew serious about crime as a way of life, and Cherokee Bill joined in the mayhem they created.

Here's a partial litany of their activities. On July 2, 1894, the Scales Mercantile in Wetumka, Creek Nation, was robbed by the gang. On July 5, the Nowata depot was robbed, and station agent Richard Richards was killed, followed by the death of Sam Collins, the conductor of the train, with both deaths attributed to Cherokee Bill. On July 14, a stagecoach between Muskogee and Fort Gibson was robbed; on July 16, a Frisco train was robbed at Red Rock; and on July 31, the bank at Chandler was robbed, and Cherokee Bill killed a local barber who raised an alarm. For four more months, stores, banks, businesses, stagecoaches and individuals were robbed; trains were wrecked and robbed; and Cherokee Bill killed another man, Ernest Melton, while robbing a store in Lenapah.

It became difficult to know if every robbery attributed to the Cook Gang was done by the men, and in the heat of gunfire, it was difficult to know who actually killed which people. In addition to men being killed, women were not exempted.

The U.S. secretary of war was outraged with the murders and robberies, which seemed beyond the control of area lawmen. He threatened that he would "abrogate the treaties, abolish the tribal relations and establish a territorial government." Rewards were posted, and lawmen were determined to obtain law and order.

Deputy U.S. Marshal Isaac Rogers is not to be confused with the son of Rabb Rogers, former slave of Clem Rogers. That Isaac Rogers reportedly also became a marshal, but what immediately rules him out is that Rabb's son lived well beyond the death of the Ike Rogers–pursuing Goldsby. Marshal Ike didn't live long enough to undergo a Dawes interview. His mother, Martha Richardson, did, and so did his son, Theodore Cooey Vann Rogers. Ike's mother's parents were reportedly Edward and Annie Humphries. The interviews reveal that Ike had been owned by Elzira May as a youngster. His wife, Sallie Vann, died at the age of twenty-four in 1884, leaving behind two young sons, Nelson Vann Rogers and Cooey. Children from an ensuing marriage to his first wife's sister, Ruthie, and then to a third wife, Sarah Fry, include Florence, Eddie and several others.

When still a teenager, Isaac joined Company E, First Kansas Infantry, during the Civil War and was mustered out at the age of eighteen. In 1884, he testified to a Congressional committee that his children were being denied an education such as that being provided by the Cherokee Nation to Indians and whites.

Cherokee Bill was sentenced to death on December 2, 1895, by Judge Isaac Parker. But the outlaw was not through with crime. In a desperate jailbreak attempt, he killed guard Lawrence Keating. Bill was executed on March 17, 1896, at the Fort Smith gallows. Interestingly, many members of the public believed that Ike Rogers had insidiously betrayed a fellow black Cherokee in order to benefit from collecting the posted reward. Ike Rogers was cold-bloodedly shot to death by Cherokee Bill's brother, Clarence Goldsby, on April 21, 1897, in Fort Gibson.

William Lee Starr's interview continued: "Clarence went to St. Louis and enlisted in the army and when discharged he was employed in the Pullman service until he died. His body was shipped from St. Louis to the Indian Territory and he was buried at Fort Gibson, his hometown."

The Wild West was indeed a reality, fueled by the trauma of the Civil War, uprooted people and a depressed, although rejuvenating, economy in which large sums of money would be known to flow through hardscrabble areas, baiting down-and-out young men.

References

Boydstun, Q.B. *Growing Up with Oklahoma.* N.p.: Oklahoma Historical Society, 1982.

Dawes Roll documents, Fold 3, as well as Find-a-Grave and WPA Indian-Pioneer papers.

Shirley, Glenn. *Marauders of the Indian Nations: The Bill Cook Gang and Cherokee Bill.* Stillwater, OK: Barbed Wire Press, 1994.

Smith, Nicka. Who Is Nicka Smith? www.whoisnickasmith.com.

West, C.W. Dub. *Outlaws and Peace Officers of Indian Territory.* N.p.: Muskogee Publishing Company, 1987.

CHAPTER 13

WILL ROGERS'S CHILDHOOD MENTORS

Karen Coody Cooper

Will Rogers—beloved Cherokee son, vaudeville star, motion picture actor, political pundit and columnist—earned a spot in the hearts of Americans for his wit and down-home humor and as a kind-hearted, kindred soul during hard times. He was born on November 4, 1879, on a vast, lonely Cherokee ranch.

How did he become the singular, well-grounded person he became? There were several influences during Will's childhood at the Rogers ranch on the Verdigris River in the Cherokee Nation. According to the editors of the book *The Papers of Will Rogers*, volume 1, "The young Rogers learned by watching and imitating Dan Walker, an African American cowboy and top roper, who was considered the head cowhand on the Rogers ranch."

Dan Walker, a Cherokee Freedman, was among the best ropers and riders in the area, and Will spent many pleasant hours with Dan and Dan's children learning those skills. The Oklahoma Historical Society posted Walker's biography on its website. Walker's birthdate is cited as circa 1852.

Will's father, Clement Vann Rogers, was a well-known and successful Cherokee citizen born in 1839. He was primarily a no-nonsense businessman. Clement's mother had deeded her newly grown son several head of cattle, some horses and two slaves formerly owned by Clement's deceased father. The two black men, Rabb and Houston, had established the ranch's crops.

Will's mother was of German-Welsh-Cherokee descent. Mary America Schrimsher brought grace to a ranch household in an unruly territory.

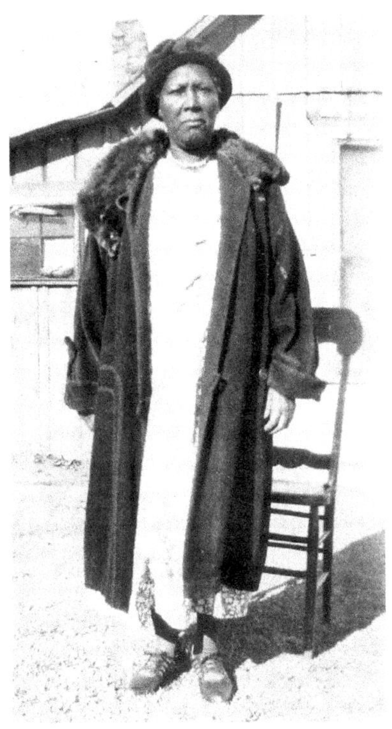

Left: Agnes "Babe" Walker served as a surrogate mother for young Will Rogers following his mother's death. *Will Rogers Memorial Museum and Home.*

Below: A black coachman drives past the house where Will Rogers was born and spent his childhood. *Will Rogers Memorial Museum and Home.*

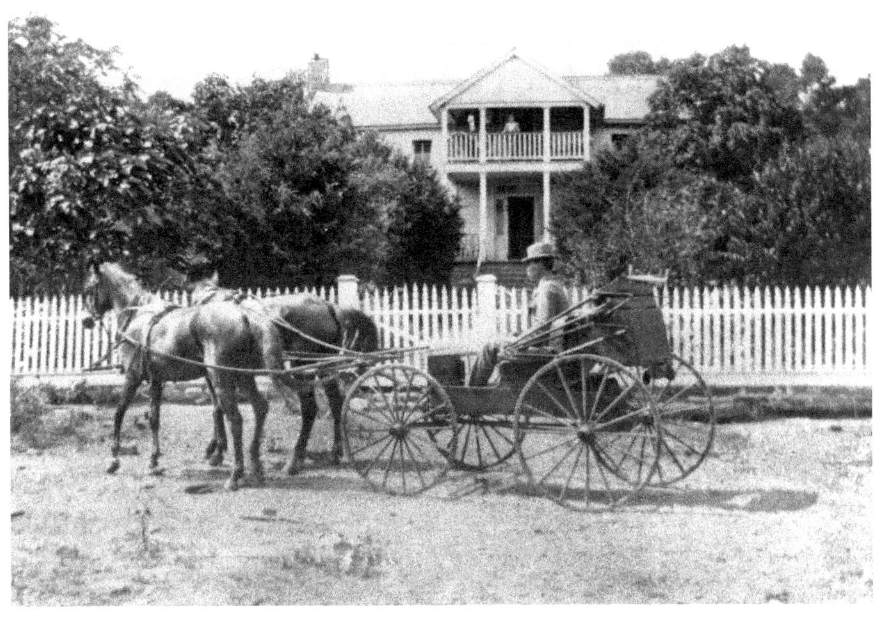

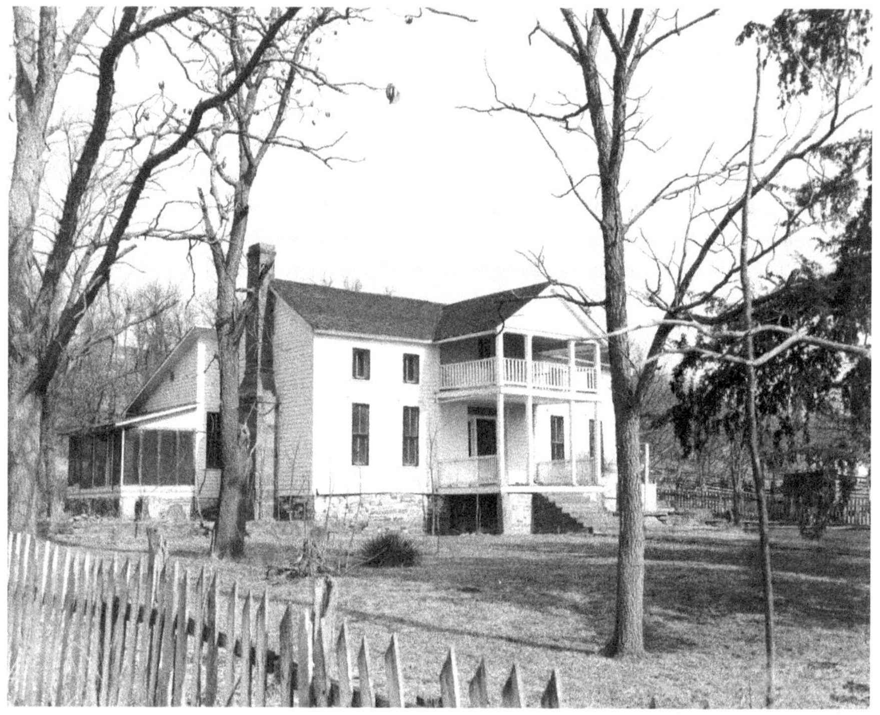

The childhood home of Will Rogers was large but simple, and it was moved in the '60s before man-made Lake Oologah flooded the original area. *Will Rogers Memorial Museum and Home.*

She was noted for being lively and full of humor. During the Civil War, Clem became a soldier, having to abandon the ranch to ruin. It became necessary for Rabb to escort Mary Schrimsher and her infant daughter to safety with her parents in Tahlequah. Eventually, she was forced to take refuge in Texas out of harm's way. Slaves scattered, and at war's end, they were free and in need of a livelihood. Many returned to their former locations, hoping to find employment. Clem returned to rebuild his ranch and employed the black families he trusted and admired. When young Will was born, Agnes Walker and her mother, Sidney, were rushed to the Rogers home to assist with the birth.

When Will Rogers's mother died in 1890, young Will was only ten years old and found solace at the home of "Uncle Dan" and his wife, "Aunt Babe" (Agnes Walker), along with their children closest to his age: Charlotte, Charlie and Mack. The area was sparsely populated, and Will's childhood friends were primarily the Walker children, as well as the large family of

Babe's uncle, Charles Rabb Rogers, a renowned storyteller who enthralled the young Cherokee boy and likely influenced Will's glibness. Will hunted and fished with the families, ate in their homes and worked alongside them as he matured. Will Rogers reported, "I was raised by them."

Most of the Rogerses' former slaves lived out their lives with the Rogers surname. The two Freedmen families were headed by half brothers, sharing the same slave mother, Lucy Rogers, originally owned by Robert Rogers and passed on to Clem along with her sons.

Rabb Rogers had been born in about 1830, and his father had been slave Jesse Rowe, owned by probably Dick or Dave Rowe. It is likely that Rabb's parents became separated due to living with different owners. Jesse Rowe is later found in Texas with a different wife and a different owner, George Starr.

Rabb met wife Rhoda, a former slave of Jim McCoy from the Choctaw Nation, during the war. She had been born circa 1844, and they married after achieving freedom, having met at Fort Gibson, where hundreds of black families from various area tribes had been harbored during the war. She identified her parents as Sam and Amanda Perry and testified in 1905 that she had made application as a Choctaw Freedman but preferred to enroll with the Cherokees due to her marriage. Rabb noted that Rhoda claimed her father had bought her freedom from McCoy. She renounced a Choctaw enrollment in order to be listed as Cherokee by adoption.

The children born to the couple were Nick (born in 1868), Jack (circa 1869), Houston Rogers Jr. (circa 1872), Clem (born in 1874), Jasper (born in 1876), Clara, Lucy (born circa 1878), Isaac/Ike (circa 1880), Grace (circa 1880), Margaret (circa 1883) and Rose/Rosie. Ike grew up to become a deputy U.S. marshal, as was Dan Walker.

Houston Rogers Sr., a half brother of Rabb, was born in about 1840. His father was named Shoo Cow, and when reporting the name, Houston told interview auditors that he expected them to laugh. Shoo Cow, deceased at the time the record was made, is listed with the word *Freedman* in the column for "Father." Shoo Cow's name is listed in the "Owner" column. Shoo Cow had either been born free or was freed before the Civil War, or his son Houston was uncertain of the information. Houston's mother was listed as former slave Lucy Rogers (the same mother as Rabb's).

Houston's wife, Sidney/Sydney Ross, was born in about 1860, according to the listing on the Freedmen Roll. Ensuing interview records suggest that she had died some time before the roll was composed, and it is possible that her age at death had been noted on the later roll and therefore an estimated birth year could not accurately be estimated from her age as listed on the roll. Sidney was noted on Freedman records as having been fathered by Cherokee Indian John Brown, and no listing of her mother's name was provided, although the absent mother was noted as having been owned by Oliver Ross, son of Andrew Ross (youngest brother of Chief John Ross). Interestingly, the editors of *The Papers of Will Rogers* mentioned in the book's biographical appendix that Sidney Ross was the daughter of a full-blood Cherokee mother and an African American father. Apparently, the source for that statement is a 1938 interview with Houston's daughter Agnes/Aggie (born on December 8, 1862, at Fort Gibson in Indian Territory) in which she reported her maternal grandmother to be full-blood Cherokee and her grandfather "a negro." If Sidney's birth date was circa 1860, Sidney could not be the birth mother of Agnes in 1862. Sidney's sons were all born a decade later: Samuel and Rufus O. Rogers born in about 1873, Charles in 1875, Eli in 1877, Robert (Bud) in 1880 and Anderson circa 1882—all plausible dates, given that the early dates are estimates, for Sidney to have delivered babies. Agnes's mother was apparently someone other than Sidney, yet she appears to be talking about Sidney as her mother (adoptive perhaps). In any case, it appears that Sidney's sons had a Cherokee ancestor.

Half brothers Rabb and Houston are said to have supported opposite sides during the war. At war's end, Clem Rogers reportedly sent for Rabb and Houston and said to them, "Well, Rabb's side won. My side lost. I would like for you to work for me." The two families were provided with land, and Rabb built a two-story frame house of seven rooms in a locust tree grove. The creek there became known as Rabb's Creek. Houston's house was a one-room log cabin with a log summer kitchen.

When Will Rogers was big enough to have a working horse, his father bought Comanche, a cream-colored trained cow pony, from Houston Rogers's son Anderson Rogers. The pony was branded "AR" on one shoulder. Will and Comanche bonded, and the horse helped Rogers win several racing and roping events. Comanche accompanied Will on the road in Wild West shows. A New York gentleman offered $500 for Comanche after seeing him perform, but Rogers said, "There is not money enough in that grandstand to buy old Comanche."

Will recalled that he was five years old before he saw a white child. The families of Houston Rogers, Rabb Rogers and Dan Walker were lifelong friends of Will's, and Will continued seeing them whenever he returned home.

Will's father was involved in politics and appreciated the help of Rabb and Houston to bring in black votes during election periods. Houston's home had a large picnic grounds used for annual community gatherings. Dan Walker also served as a deputy U.S. marshal. Agnes had attended a one-room Cherokee school on Rabb's Creek. She worked as a cook for Clem's household and later as cook for the Talala Hotel.

Rabb died on January 31, 1922, and is buried at Hickory Creek Cemetery in Nowata, Oklahoma. His wife, Rhoda, died on August 27, 1913, and is buried at the same cemetery. Daughter Rose was named executor of Rabb's estate of eleven lots of land and a dwelling in the Cassity Place addition of Nowata valued at $750.

Another cemetery exists south of Acuff's Bluff where a Jessie Rogers was buried in 1876 at the age of nine, along with an unnamed infant who died in February 1882. It is believed that Houston and members of his family are buried at the unnamed cemetery located on a ranch recently owned by Todd Fugate. The last burial occurred in 1918, when Bud Rogers's daughter died of flu.

Aside from consulting public records, most of the previous information and more can be found in the first volume (1879–1904) of *The Papers of Will Rogers*.

References

Ancestry.com, online access to census, rolls, Find-a-Grave and Fold 3 papers.

Burton, Art. "Walker, Daniel." Encyclopedia of Oklahoma History and Culture. Oklahoma Historical Society website, viewed April 2016.

McDowell, Alene D. Agnes Walker Interview. Indian-Pioneer Papers, University of Oklahoma, 1938.

Wertheim, Arthur Frank, and Barbara Bair. *The Papers of Will Rogers*. Vol. 1, *November 1879–1904*. Norman: University of Oklahoma Press, 1996.

CHAPTER 14

THE COLORED HIGH SCHOOL OF THE CHEROKEE NATION

T.L. Ballenger

Excerpted with permission from Chronicles of Oklahoma *30, no. 4 (1952): 454–62.*

About six miles northwest of Tahlequah on a little knoll overlooking two of the most beautiful springs of clear sparkling water in Eastern Oklahoma are to be found the ruins of a forgotten enterprise of the Cherokee Nation. On this spot once lived a slaveholder named Webber.

The Nation had primary schools which the Negro could attend but, for a long time, no provision was made for his higher training. The Cherokees had had their two well organized and well conducted seminaries for high education of their own boys and girls for over forty years before any provision was made for the higher education of the colored people, former slaves and their children, in the Nation.

Some advocates of the rights of the Cherokee freedman doubtless had a sincere interest in his educational advancement and urged the Nation to provide facilities for it. Had the needs of the Negro not fitted in with the ambitions of a political party, the humanitarian element alone might never had accomplished their desires. Up to near the last decade of the Nineteenth Century the National Party in the Cherokee Nation had been predominantly successful in keeping the reins of government firmly in its hands. The Downing Party saw in the Negro school question an opportunity to win the vote of the Negroes and their Cherokee sympathizers, and was not slow to take advantage of its opportunity. This is not the only case in American

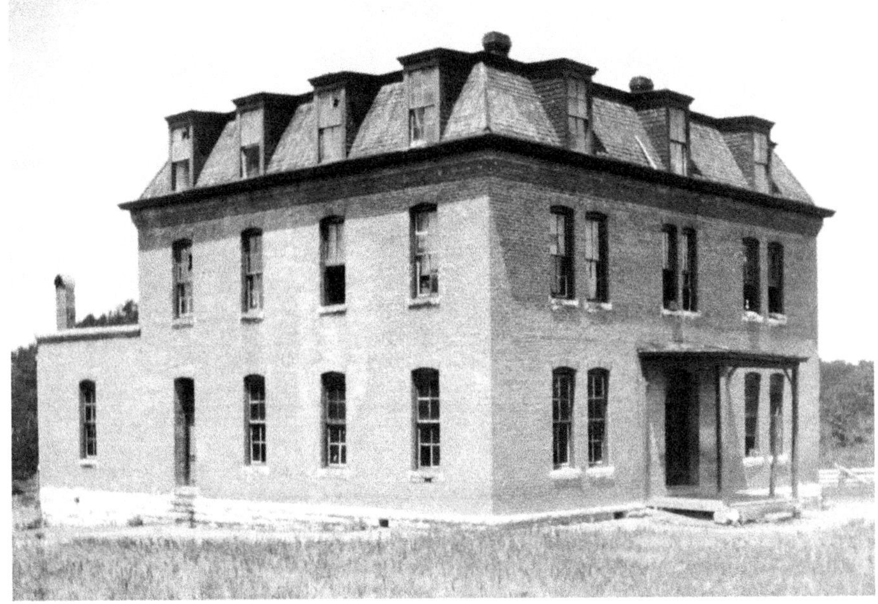

The Cherokee Colored High School opened in 1890 at Double Springs, northwest of Tahlequah. *Northeastern State University Archives.*

history of a political party's bidding for the Negro vote. The Downing party made the establishment of a high school for the colored people the chief issue of its campaign in the fall of 1887, and won. Hence, with the inauguration of Joel B. Mayes in January, 1888, the administration was pledged to establish for the Negro people an educational institution where their children could go beyond the mere rudiments of a primary education.

With the election of the Downing Party governmental machinery was immediately set in motion for the construction of a high school building. In November, 1888, the Cherokee National Council authorized its erection and appropriated $10,000 to pay for it. Two strong springs furnished an excellent water supply for such an institution, and it was surrounded by a valley well adapted to agriculture and horticulture. The citizens of Tahlequah raised a fund of four hundred dollars to pay for the improvements already on this site.

The main building was to be 48 x 50 feet with kitchen and dining room 16 x 50 feet, three stories high, made of good brick, with a stone foundation, and shingle, mansard and metal roof. A cellar was constructed under a part of the building. It contained about twenty rooms. The first floor consisted of a living room, a dining room and kitchen, a storeroom, an office, and a schoolroom. The second floor was used mainly for the girls' quarters, and the third floor for the boys. A somewhat comprehensive list of furnishings was included in the specifications suitable for general housekeeping and dormitory purposes. The bricks for the building were burned a short distance east of the site of the structure. The building was erected in the year 1889 and was ready for occupancy January 1, 1890.

The laws of the Cherokee Nation placed the school under the general supervision of the Superintendent of Education, along with that of the Cherokee male and female seminaries. The Superintendent of Education was superseded, a little later, by a Board of Education, consisting of three members....The school year was to consist of two terms, one of twenty weeks and the other of sixteen weeks. Each pupil paid five dollars per month for board. This payment was raised in 1893 to seven dollars and fifty cents. It was the duty of the steward to see that the money was paid. If any student failed to pay, the law instructed the Superintendent to dismiss him from school. The average attendance had to be kept up to twenty-five under penalty of discontinuance of the school.

The total appropriation for this school ranged from $2,000 to $3,000 a year. The steward of the Colored High School was appointed and commissioned by the Principal Chief for a period of two years with the advice and consent of the Senate. He had to be a citizen of the Cherokee Nation, though the teachers did not....His salary was three hundred dollars a year. The school was to run two years with twenty-five pupils, then twenty-five more were to be added. At the end of four years the first twenty-five were to be discharged and the number was to be kept at fifty from then on.

The school first opened for business January 1, 1890, with Nelson Lowrey of Tahlequah as steward and with an enrollment of approximately twenty-five pupils. Lowrey served in this capacity until November 26, 1895 and then served again during the years 1902 and 1903....O.S. Fox of Ohio was principal teacher from 1890 to 1894. Only one teacher was employed at first, later as many as three or four. Mrs. Fannie Lowrey was teacher during a part of her husband's term, 1895–1896, and then taught there at intervals for a number of years afterwards. Originally from Ft. Scott, Kansas, she was one of the oldest colored teachers, in point of service, in the Nation, having taught in the high school and in the public schools practically all of her life. She died at Tahlequah in 1928.

Mrs. Clara Vann, grandmother of Mrs. Lelia Ross of Tahlequah, was matron and laundress at the school in those early years. George Vann was appointed steward November 26, 1895 and served until August 25, 1899.

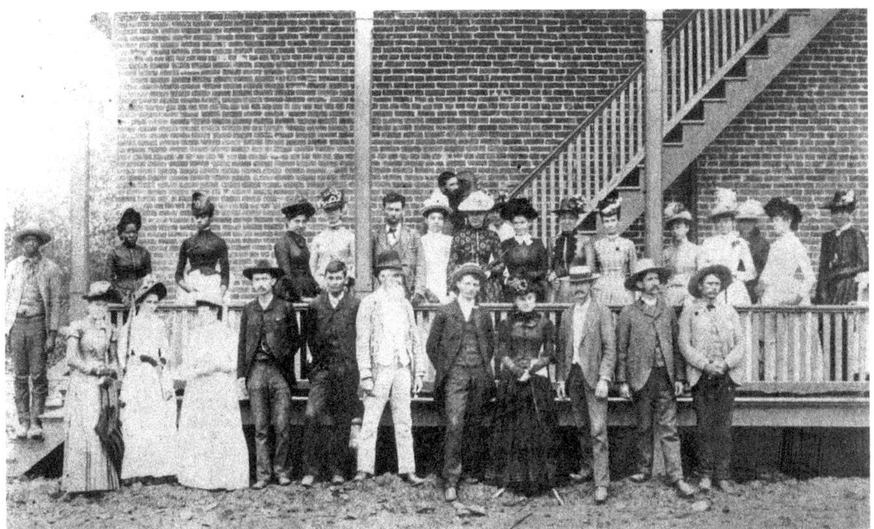

Above: Attendees of a teaching institute in the Cherokee Nation before statehood included Fannie Lowrey, one of the black women on the left. *Northeastern State University Archives.*

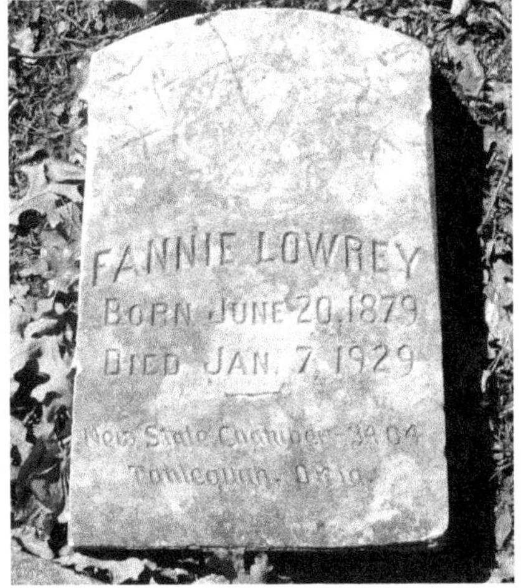

Right: Fannie Jones Lowrey, interred at Stick Ross Cemetery, Tahlequah, taught in Fort Gibson schools before marrying Cherokee Colored High School steward Nelson Lowery. *Jim Roaix.*

Evidently the high school attendance was not maintained at its legal maximum for, after a few years, it was considered advisable to establish a primary department.

George F. Nave was steward from August, 1899 to November, 1901.... Mrs. L.T. Brown [was] the teacher. Superintendent Nave submitted [a] report in which he listed thirteen primary pupils whose fathers were able to pay and fifteen who were orphans or had no means of support. These first thirteen came from Chouteau, Spavinaw, Vinita, Melvin, and Hayden. The residences of the others are not given. The pupils were required to work one hour each day at some useful employment about the school.

The graduating class of 1908 consisted of Lelia C. Swepston, now Lelia Ross of Tahlequah, Katie Glass, Roscoe Foreman, and Clarence Hicks.

By act of Congress April 30, 1908, the Secretary of the Interior was instructed to take charge of all buildings and lands of the Cherokees used for government, school, or other tribal purposes, appraise and sell the property, and deposit the proceeds in the United States Treasury to the credit of the Cherokee Nation. In compliance with this Congressional act this property was sold at auction to the highest bidder, the Collate Missionary Baptist Association {colored}, for $1,350. Chief W.C. Rogers turned it over to them and gave them a deed to it April 3, 1914....The Negroes had a hard time raising this purchase price and eventually the amount was reduced some four hundred dollars.

In July of 1916 the building was burned, possibly a case of incendiarism. The land was sold by this Association to private individuals in 1920.

The memory of it reminds one of the many excellent enterprises of the Cherokee Nation, not a failure but a stepping stone to better conditions. It lasted for two decades and was evidently of considerable value to the colored people of the Cherokee Nation.

From KCC: Following the Civil War, parents of black children organized subscription schools, often held in their churches. Two black schools were planned by the Cherokee superintendent of education in March 1869 to be at Tahlequah and on Fourteen Mile Creek in Tahlequah District. During a Congressional hearing in the 1880s, black parents pressured the Cherokee Nation to provide a high school for their children. In 1895, "Fourteen primary schools were for the use of the negro citizens of the Nation, besides

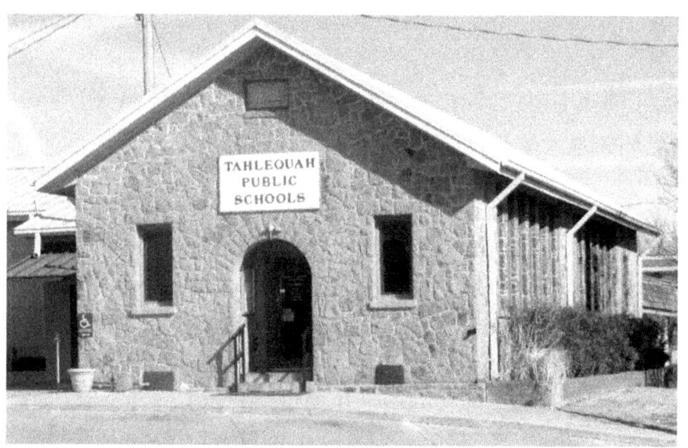

Former Lincoln Negro School in Tahlequah dates from 1937–38 and currently houses the administrative offices of Tahlequah Public Schools. *Jim Roaix.*

which they had a fine high school, kept up, like all the others, at the expense of the Cherokee government," wrote James Mooney in *Myths of the Cherokee.* In June 1900, the Female Seminary had 140 participants in the first summer normal school (the term for teacher training), and 22 African Americans attended a normal school held at the Colored High School. The current administrative offices of the Tahlequah Public Schools are housed in the former Lincoln Negro School on Water Avenue, dating from 1937–38.

CHAPTER 15

OILMAN, EDUCATOR, PAMPHLETEER

GEORGE F. NAVE

Mark A. Harrison

Excerpted with permission from author's research.

George F. Nave, born in Neosho Falls, Kansas in 1864, witnessed the end of the institution of chattel slavery within both the Cherokee Nation and the United States. His father, Washington (Wash) Nave, mother Mariah, and four children are found on the 1865 Kansas State Census because the family fled north to Kansas from Indian Territory during the Civil War, as had many others. George's father was noted as a farmer, and his father's birth location, along with the three oldest children, was recorded as Cherokee Nation. Their surname came from Wash having been a slave of Cherokee Mary Nave. Mary's daughter, Jane Pack, was noted in Dawes Commission testimony as having been the owner of Mariah.

Washington Nave, Sr. enlisted and served during the war with the Colored Kansas Infantry Militia, the first black unit to engage Confederate Troops. These units took the fight to the Confederacy by setting up defensive forts in Kansas and patrolling other states such as Arkansas, and even invading Indian Territory and liberating Fort Gibson. On October 29, 1862, a skirmish occurred at Island Mound, Missouri with a unit of Confederate guerrillas that resulted in the first combat death of black soldiers in the Civil War. This was the first engagement between Colored Troops and Confederates. Other notable battles these Troops were credited with include: Cabin Creek, Cherokee Nation, Jul 1 and 2, 1863; Honey Springs, Indian Territory, Jul 17, 1863; Lawrence, Kansas, Jul 27, 1863; Horse-Head Creek, Arkansas, Feb 17, 1864; Roseville Creek, Arkansas, Mar 20, 1864; Prairie D'Ann, Arkansas, Apr 13, 1864; Poison Springs, Arkansas, Apr 18, 1864; Jenkins' Ferry, Arkansas, Apr 30, 1864; Fort Gibson, Cherokee Nation, Sep 16, 1864; Timber Creek, Cherokee Nation, Nov 19, 1864; Joy's Ford, Arkansas, Jan 8, 1865; and Clarksville, Arkansas, Jan 18, 1865. In short the efforts of these troops allowed the Union Armies to focus their attention further east and south.

The 1890 CN Census of the Saline District shows that Wash Sr. and George were listed as farmers with 45 acres of land under cultivation and improvements listed at $120.00 in value. There were 8 horses and 94 Cattle and 35 hogs listed as their holdings. By 1907 this "in common land usage" would come to an end as all recognized citizens of the Cherokee Nation were given individual land allotments.

During the early 1890s Dave Nave, an older brother of George, came under the scrutiny of Law Enforcement when he was arrested for hiring a white man to work on his property without obtaining a permit. For this offense he was sentenced to six-months in the Cherokee Penitentiary or a fifty-six dollar fine. George was paying attention. During his Dawes Commission citizenship hearing he presented a permit he had obtained to hire a white man. This permit served to confirm his rights to Cherokee citizenship at that time since only citizens of the Nation were required to report and purchase those permits.

On February 3, 1898 an announcement in the *Indian Chieftain* newspaper of Vinita, IT noted, "George F. Nave was appointed to teach at the Brush Creek School." In November 1899, Nave was appointed by Principal Chief T.M. Buffington to the position of Steward of the Colored High School in Tahlequah. That appointment was to last for a period of two years. As late as June 22, 1901 Nave served as Superintendent.

Nave married Emma Hudson, daughter of William Hudson of Fort Gibson in September of 1899. Their marriage announcement was published in the *Fort Gibson Post.*

Based on George Nave's employment and later business expertise it is assumed he received a higher academic education than the majority. It's possible his education was obtained at the Lincoln Institute, Jefferson City, Missouri, which first provided teacher training in 1870, or at Quindaro Freedman's School, near Kansas City, Kansas which began offering teacher training in 1872. The 1920 census finds George's daughter Margaret studying at Wilberforce University in Ohio. That school had been founded in 1856 and perhaps George had studied there.

J. Milton Turner, a Missouri educator was named by President Grant as the first African American diplomat to represent the United States in a foreign country as Ambassador to Liberia (1871–78). Turner was successful in securing $75,000 in federal funds to assist Afro-Cherokee people, and Nave was tasked with conducting paralegal services preparing the cases of Freedmen involved in disputes with the Dawes Commission. Both men became noted entrepreneurs and civil rights advocates within Indian Territory and later the State of Oklahoma.

During their work, the validity of the Kern and Clifton rolls arose. Nave gave testimony to Inspector William J. McConnell: "George Nave, a freedmen and schoolteacher from Choteau testified that he had observed Kern collecting fees from the freedmen during the payments. However, Nave's testimony dealt more with the activities of others. He claimed at Fort Gibson he saw armed men seize freedmen after they had received a check and take them into a room where collectors representing the trader Severs were sitting. He saw two white men forcibly search Rufus Mackey and Elijah Coody of Braggs in an effort to collect for Severs. If a freedman refused to pay, Nave claimed that he was put in jail at Muskogee. Among those jailed for failing to pay were Rabbit Sanders of Fort Gibson and Rufus Mackey. Sanders, who had given his check to Hannah Mayfield of Muskogee, was kept in jail until the check was produced."

Meanwhile, Nave was interviewed by the Dawes Commission on June 22, 1901 applying for himself and his eight-month old daughter Peggy (Margaret). He reported that his wife Emma (Hudson) had died. Nave had in his possession their marriage certificate. His testimony stated that his parents had been deceased for several years. On this date of testimony he and several of his siblings were called upon to verify each of their testimonies.

By March of 1904 George F. Nave had become one of the principal stockholders of the Muskogee Oil and Gas Company, where he also attained the position of general manager. He went on to encourage other Freedmen to invest in this endeavor. On March 15th 1904 a group of colored businessmen were noted in the local newspaper as "putting up a derrick." With locally issued permits and the acquired machinery on hand they begin drilling at once. On June 21st 1904, with two wells operated by the company, they had saved 100 barrels of this valuable crude oil. Two months later a change in the board of directors suddenly placed George F. Nave as the chief executive officer of the Muskogee Oil

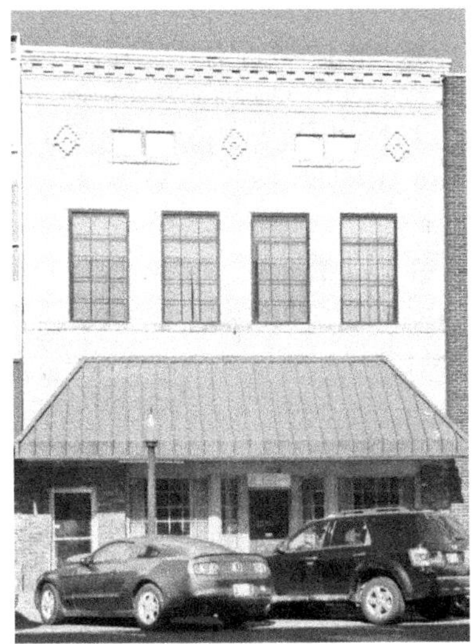

George F. Nave's oil company had offices in this building at 208 Broadway in Muskogee. *Jim Roaix.*

and Gas Company. The company later brought storage tanks to Muskogee with the capacity of holding over 100 barrels of crude oil.

Promotion of their company read as follows: "As ours is the only Negro Company in the world owning and controlling profitable oil wells, we congratulate you again on having cast your lot with us, and remind you that in the great Indian Territory Ethiopa [*sic*] has stretched up her heart unto God and stretched forth her hand into the commercial problems of the world. We shipped our first car load of oil July 4, 1904." The address of Muskogee Oil and Gas Company was 208 1-2 Broadway, Muskogee, Indian Territory. George F. Nave was listed in the city directory in 1905 as manager of the company with address at 409 North Sixth Street.

On May 12, 1912, Nave applied for and was permitted to build a $2,500 home at 225 West Southside Boulevard in Muskogee. He lived the remainder of his life in the home, upon occasion taking in a boarder or two. His daughter also lived with him after she divorced, and apparently had no children.

In 1917, George F. Nave responded to President Wilson's call to war with his own pamphlet, "The New Negro's Attitude Toward His Government." The subtitle is "He Will Not Prove a Traitor to the Cause of His Country Nor a Coward in the Face of Its Enemies." The address for the publication is noted as 201 Love Building, Muskogee, Oklahoma. From 1913 through 1916, the Muskogee Colored Library was also housed in the Love Building.

The *Muskogee Times* ran the headline "Creek Girl Charges her Guardian Appropriated $1525 From Her Estate" on Sept 2, 1918. The story cited, "Charge that George F. Nave, her guardian, and W.H. Dewalt, conspired to misappropriate $1,525 of the funds of her estate, in 1910, are made in a suit by Rella Bruner, Creek freedman, against Nave and Dewalt, filed in district court today. The girl's allotment was sold on August 1, 1910, to Dewalt for $2,615 according to the petition. On December 8, 1910, she charged Nave and Dewalt misappropriated $1,526 of it."

Bruner had been an infant when first assigned to Nave. At least one other litigant, Levi Webber, also filed a suit. Guardians could generally cite expenses they incurred in serving these vulnerable clients, yet sometimes the land that was sold to provide needed funds for the children also served to benefit the business interests of the guardian.

In the 1936 Muskogee city directory, George's daughter Margaret Nave was listed as a welfare worker while her father was listed as a realtor, and in 1938 she was noted in the directory as a teacher while her father continued as a realtor. Nave died Jan. 15, 1939 and is buried in the Booker T. Washington Cemetery in Muskogee.

References

Ballenger, T.L. "The Colored High School of the Cherokee Nation." *Chronicles of Oklahoma* 30, no. 4 (1952).

Carter, Michael E., Major. *First Kansas Colored Volunteers*. N.p.: Pickle Partners Publishing, 2015.

Conditions on Indian Affairs. United States Senate, vol. 2, circa 1886. Library of Congress, Washington, D.C.

Cornsilk, David. Writings and conversations.

Dawes Commission records, Indian Territory. National Archives, Washington, D.C.

Grayson, Eli. Various conversations.

Lambert, Mary. "Re: H.W. Twine." MBA, Webster University, Kansas City, Missouri, 2000.

Littlefield, Daniel F. *The Cherokee Freedmen*. N.p.: Greenwood Press, 1978.

Littlefield, Daniel F., and Lonnie E. Underhill. "Black Dreams and 'Free' Homes: The Oklahoma Territory, 1891–1894." *Phylon* 34, no. 4 (1973). Clark Atlanta University.

McRae, Bennie J., Jr. *First Kansas Colored Infantry Regiment*. N.p.: Lest We Forget Publications, July 1994.

Nave, George F. *The New Negro's Attitude Towards His Government*. Pamphlet, 1917.

Various historic newspaper articles.

CHAPTER 16

THE NEW NEGRO'S ATTITUDE TOWARD HIS GOVERNMENT

George F. Nave

From a pamphlet published in 1917 in Muskogee.

When the last regular session of the state legislature of the State of Oklahoma adjourned without attaching an "illiteracy test" amendment to some of the questions to be submitted to the voters of the state, it was taken for granted by all, that in due course of time with a broad and liberal public school system such as is inaugurated in Oklahoma, Texas and several other Southern States, there would not be any illiterate voters. When the time comes that an education is considered more valuable than the gathering of a crop of cotton, and we have eight months of school in the counties and nine months in the cities each year for all children of scholastic age, illiteracy will disappear and we will have one strong united body of intelligent citizens as worthy exponents of a great and free country—one of the things which the New Negro in the United States of America stands for. Then there will be no North nor no South, no white man's country, no black man's country nor no red man's country, but one strong united country of all its people, and for all of its people alike.

And since the time has come when the public mind requires concrete instead of abstract expressions; since it is necessary that he who condemns a prevailing policy must recommend a better one, the New Negro, besides telling what he stands for should also tell what he wants, what he expects and

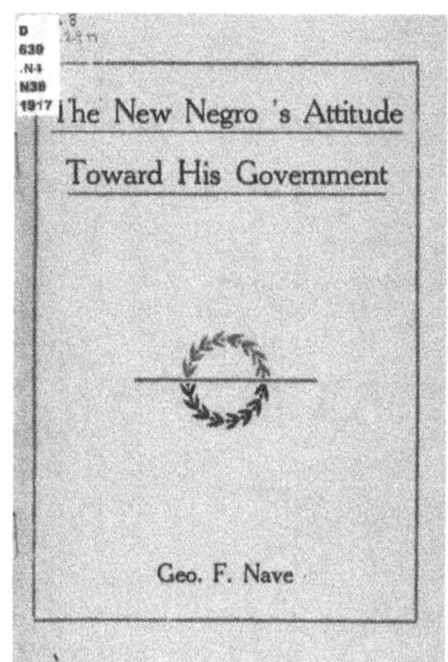

George F. Nave, former principal of the Colored High School, published a patriotic pamphlet in Muskogee in 1917. *Jim Roaix.*

what he asks for in times of peace and in times of war. When the Honorable Mr. Charles E. Hughes, in speaking to a Colored audience, said, "I am sure you don't want particular things done for you on account of Color," with a negative inference, he put down a rock upon which every American Negro in the United States should build his house of determination.

No, the Negro is not asking special acts of government nor state for his special benefit. He is no longer a child and a ward. Fifty years of freedom, fifty years of actual contact with the business world, fifty years of commercial activity and education, have enabled him to develop into a full grown man.

And he wants only a chance to play a man's part in the material construction of things. He wants a chance to earn an honest living along all avenues and channels that are open to other men and women of his skill and ability.

He wants to bear the burdens as well as enjoy the blessings of his country. He will not claim a country when it is enjoying peace and plentitude, and desert it in times of war and devastation.

He wants fairness in every particular, and justice everywhere; in the courts, upon the lands, and upon the high seas; can he ask for more, and should he ask for less?

He wants to shed his blood along with the blood of other citizens, when the shedding of blood is required to preserve and protect his country.

He expects to give his life along with the lives of other loyal men, when life must be sacrificed to defend the flag which protects him and his fellowmen.

He expects recognition and representation in all of the trades, professions and arts commensurate with his capability to perform and maintain them. He expects to make this country accept him, claim him, and be proud of him from the valuable service he will render it. He expects the stars and stripes, the Country's Flag, to be his friend and his shield, because of the protection he will offer it in times of war. If the United States of America is to become the greatest nation in the world, there is much to be done to make it so. Great in name only and not in fact is a sham. Lasting peace without lasting strength is a phantom.

The New Negro must play in the game of making things come to pass. With steady nerve, strong muscle and resourceful brain he must compete with some, and cooperate with others.

He must not fall to the level of the Armenian, who has no country that he will defend, no flag which he will honor, no principle for which he will fight, no allies to assist him in time of war, and who is driven from place to place by the ill winds of fate like cattle to the slaughter pens, and dies without a struggle and is buried in an unmarked grave.

He cannot afford to stand idly by and let someone else do all of the work in building up a great nation. The soil must be nourished, fertilized and scientifically tilled. The railroad systems must be enlarged and extended. Forts must be well fortified, harbors must be guarded, canals must be cut; munitions factories must be erected and maintained; a strong merchant marine must be built up; an efficient army and navy must be prepared; aircrafts must be made and operated, and undersea vessels and wireless telegraph stations must be owned and controlled by the government of the United States. The soldiers upon the firing line must be fed, their families at home must be provided for, and their children made orphans by the ravages of war must be protected and cared for.

The New Negro must and will contribute largely to the full development of all of the resources and defenses of this wonderful country, which is now and will continue to be his home and in which he has reared his families, buried his dead and educated his youth. With the president of our Republic declaring before the Congress of the United States of America "that we are at war" against the imperial government of Germany, with the war clouds hovering over him, with flags fluttering all around him, with the call to enlistment resounding in his ears, with the fire of patriotism burning upon every altar, what does the New Negro ask? Does he ask to be let along, does he ask to be exempt from service, does he ask to shirk a duty that devolves upon him by virtue of his citizenship, can he ask for a share of the spoils when he has taken no part in the efforts that bring victory?

With the prospects of long life, happiness and pleasure on one side and the possibility of an early death and a soldier's grave on the other, what does the New Negro ask of his country today? Does he ask to be considered as a child in times of struggle and strife, and as a man in times of peace and tranquility? Does he ask to put the burden of upholding the honor and dignity of the people of the United States of America upon the shoulders of some one else? Does he ask that some other person now bear the brunt of the battles in defending a country in which he is equally interested and in which he has lived and prospered?

Does he ask that some one else fight all the battles necessary to hold intact a government, the life and operations of which will benefit him and his posterity? Does he claim allegiance to some other country as a fatherland? No! The New Negro will not prove a traitor to the cause of his country nor a coward in the face of its enemies. He asks that merit and manhood be made the standard of measure for all men; he asks no favors of any one because he is black nor condemnation because he isn't white.

He asks that his country appreciate his general worth, that it depend upon his ability and endurance, that it trust his honesty, that it believe in his integrity and that it call upon him, when a man is needed to do a man's work in a man's way.

CHAPTER 17

MARY WALKER ELLIOTT

WHO'S YOUR DADDY, WHERE'S YOUR MAMA?

Karen Coody Cooper

Robert Elliott, twenty-eight-year-old Cherokee citizen, visited the Dawes Commission office in Fort Gibson on August 30, 1900. After a short interview conducted by a single agent named Needles, who found Elliott's name on the 1880 enumeration as well as on the 1896 list, Elliott was approved as a Cherokee citizen by blood. The one-page Dawes interview recorded Elliott saying of his wife, Mary, "She is a Cherokee; the last census they put her on the Freedmen roll." He tried to open a window of opportunity for the interviewer to enact a change of Mary's status. Elliott cited his wife's father as having been Jack Walker (a known deceased Cherokee) and said that her mother was Polly Ross (a known Freedman).

At the end of the short interview, Commissioner Needles is reported by the transcriber to have advised Elliott "to let his wife apply for herself and the children." This suggestion might have come about due to the fact that Elliott was the stepfather of two of Mary's sons, born to Jim French, who was dead and happened to have been an outlaw. Elliott was himself the father of Mary's most recent son at the time of his making this application. The agent perhaps wanted to get firsthand information regarding the stepsons, but he should have enrolled Elliott's son as Cherokee by blood.

When Mary Walker Elliott visited the commission office on April 25, 1901, eight months later, she corroborated that her mother was "Polly Nivens" (same person as Polly Ross) and that Jack Walker, Cherokee, was her father. There would have been need of more corroboration regarding Mary's claim of being the daughter of Jack Walker. The unexpected result, however, is not that she was retained on the Freedman roll but rather that her sons, born of verifiable Cherokee fathers, were subsequently also enrolled as Freedmen. A serious transgression occurred regarding the family, as no doubt happened to many other families. Interviewers were inclined to place anyone with a seeming trace of black blood on the Freedman list regardless of testimony. While mis-assigning people did not happen in every instance, it did happen.

On December 2, 1914, more than thirteen years later, we learn from the *Muskogee Times-Democrat* that the Elliott children had been expelled from the white school they were attending (open to American Indian children but not to black children). The superintendent testified that he looked them up on the Cherokee rolls and discovered that the children were Freedmen. It is not revealed what prompted him to examine those records. Court testimony reveals that the children had no physical attributes to suggest they were black. During the trial, two of the Elliott children were asked to stand up and were described in the newspaper: "One was a handsome boy of fifteen with snappy brown eyes and a shock of dark red hair. He was the very picture of his father. The girl, a pretty gray eyed child of six, with her long straight black hair hanging down her back in braids is as perfect a specimen of an Indian as ever seen in Oklahoma." A family photograph of Mary Elliott posted on Find-a-Grave reveals her to have been a light-skinned woman with straight hair.

The newspaper report of December 5, 1914, detailed testimony at the trial:

> *Polly Ross, an aged negro woman of Fort Gibson, told of having raised Mary Walker, who is now the wife of Robert Elliott. She told of the marriage of Jack Walker, a Cherokee, and Jennie Hicks, a Cherokee girl. Mary Walker was born to them and Walker's wife then deserted him. Walker then went to the cabin of Polly Ross and employed her to raise the girl. He paid her $500 for her trouble and bought clothing for the child. The girl lived with her until she was sixteen and she married Jim French. After that she always lived with "white folks." "White folks" in this case meant whites and white-Cherokees.*

Remember that both Mary and Robert Elliott had testified before the Dawes Commission that Polly Nevins Ross was Mary's mother. The question arises: had Mary not been told until late adulthood that her actual mother was Jennie Hicks, a Cherokee, or had the story purposely been changed in order to provide access for Mary and her offspring to a white Cherokee life? Interestingly, years before, Polly had related a similar account about her own life in Eastern Cherokee application no. 18833, dated June 21, 1908, directed to Guion Miller, special commissioner of U.S. Court of Claims at Muskogee, Oklahoma. That testimony provides a duplicate of the courtroom account, except the version is about Polly herself and her parents a generation earlier:

> *My name is Polly Ross; my post office is Fort Gibson, I was born in 1843 close to Fort Gibson; I am enrolled by the Cherokees No. 147 on the Freedman roll; before the war I was living with Old man* [N]*ivens; my mother was a negro and French; my father was a Cherokee half-breed, Jack Thompson; my mother and father lived together as man and wife; my father bought my mother from Mr. [Nivens]; that was before I was born; my mother died when I was two years old and I have heard my grandmother say that my father gave Five hundred dollars for my mother; I was living with* [N]*ivens when the war broke out and until after peace was made; my father was living about five miles from Fort Gibson at that time; my grandmother was living with* [Nivens] *at that time and she was a colored woman and I was living with her.*

One of Polly's enrollment forms states that her father had been Cherokee citizen, Jack (John) Thompson, and her mother had been slave Malinda Nivens. She reported that her brother, Will Thompson, had died in the war, and she had a sister, Martha Phillips (of a different mother). Her maternal grandparents had been Nero and Sallie Smith. Her mother Malinda's siblings had been Rutha, Lilia and Patsie Smith. Witness Jonah Lewis, an acquaintance of twenty-five years, certified her to be Polly Ross and presented an account he believed true to the best of his knowledge.

During Polly's interview with the Dawes Commission, the central issue of interest became whether Polly's mother had been freed by Jack Thompson. The commission wanted to know if Polly had been born free or born a slave. Polly believed she had been born free, but there was nothing to present as written evidence. When Henry Ross (Polly's husband and stepfather to the children she raised) made application for himself and Polly as well as a grandson, he reported the boy's mother to be "Malinda Thompson," a former slave, bearing a name of great significance to Polly. The agent told Mr. Ross to tell the child's mother to enroll her own son, but apparently she never did. The commission often made demands of applicants without knowing more of the circumstances that might prevent their ability to submit applications. Ross reported that young Malinda was the child of Sarah Thompson and Ed Ross, but it is not clear which of the child's parents was the offspring of Henry and/or Polly.

To further illuminate or confound matters, there is another Freedman daughter attributed to Jack Walker and Polly Ross. Alice Walker was interviewed by Commissioner Needles of the Dawes Commission on April 24, 1901. Alice sought to enroll as a Freedman and gave the names of her parents as Jack Walker and Polly Ross, the same as Mary Walker had done. Alice did not provide details concerning her father, nor was she asked if he had been white or black. In the 1880 rolls, she was recorded as Allie Ross, and in 1896, she appeared as Alice Walker of Illinois District. When asked why she was listed as Ross, she explained that her stepfather had been a Ross. Alice provided her son's name as Samuel Benge, and he was found on a previous record as Richard Benge—same boy, changed name. Alice was asked to obtain proof of birth of her daughter (May or Mary), and from that form we learn that Polly was the midwife for the birth of Alice's daughter (as she had been for Mary Walker's offspring). The Dawes interview of Alice Walker and Mary Walker provide identical parental information.

The school suit served to publicly alter information about Mary. Alice, on the other hand, went quietly about her life and married white man William M. Bailey in 1904. His white children of a previous marriage, along with her two light-skinned children, apparently allowed the family to live in peace, and seemingly no one questioned Alice and her children regarding identity issues. U.S. census records noted Alice and her children to be "white."

Mary and Alice were likely to have been siblings (or half siblings, perhaps), although Alice wrote a big "X" on the form section that asked for a list of sibling names, ages and residences. The same form was either not completed by Mary, was misfiled, was destroyed or was permanently lost, so we don't know if she claimed a sibling.

A search for the mysterious Jenny Hicks leads inconclusively to the following scenario. John Osborn Walker and his wife, Lucinda Taylor, had a baby girl named Emma Jane Walker in 1855, and then Lucinda died in 1859. A slave woman probably tended to the child in Walker's household. There is a possibility that Jenny (Jane) Hicks could have taken up residence with John Walker several years later. Jane/Jenny was born circa 1850 to Aaron Hicks and a wife, who died when Jane was five. Jane was orphaned at ten when her father died and was sent to the Cherokee Orphanage. She would have been a young woman when Mary Walker was born in 1871, Alice was born in 1876, and then Jane Hicks died in December of that year while attending the Arkansas Female College. The circumstances could have been that of a young woman abandoning family to gain a formal education. With her death, she would never enter the lives of her daughters again. Slavery was over, and there would have been no one in Jack's home to tend to an infant and young children (his only claimed daughter was then grown and planning her own wedding). If Jenny had ever mentioned the trauma of being in an orphanage, Jack Walker would have sought a different situation for those offspring. He knew Polly Ross to be a midwife who could raise children. Jack did marry again, but somewhat later, to Georgianna Wilkins (we only know it was sometime before 1880, the year the census recorded them as a couple). They produced no children. Jack died in 1891, and Georgianna later married William A. Scott.

Polly Ross, said to have been a large mulatto woman, died at the age of seventy-five on July 22, 1917. The *Fort Gibson New Era* noted on the front page of the issue that Polly had been a cook for refugees at the fort during the war and was the best-known colored woman of the area. The tribute to her noted that she had been kind, with a charitable disposition.

However, there were some individuals who were not fond of Polly. On August 26, 1904, W.W. Hastings had conducted short interviews with Frank Smith, George W. Benge, McCoy Smith and Jack Walker to ask each of them, separately, if Polly Nivens Ross had a reputation for truth and veracity in the community of her residence. Frank J. Boudinot, self-appointed guardian of Cherokee rights, objected to the line of questioning, but it was allowed to proceed. The four men testified that Polly's reputation for truth was not just bad—it was notoriously bad. As a result, her accounts regarding personal relationships would be discounted, and her submission of forms as a midwife also would have become suspect to the members of the commission. The Jack Walker serving as one of the interviewees was a nephew of John Osborn Walker. He, his uncle, his parents and Thompson family members are buried at Citizens Cemetery in Fort Gibson.

Mary Walker, the focus of this report, was born on August 4, 1871, after slavery had ended. In two U.S. census records, she was recorded as "white" and, in two other years, was noted as "American Indian," probably because the head of household was Cherokee. Alice Walker wrote to Guion Miller in Washington, D.C., "I wish it was possible for you to see us and judge where our names should be. My mother has one quarter colored blood in her from her mother's side and of course that throws us all on the Freedman roll, while she doesn't look it at all. My father was a Cherokee…he had left my mother and taken up with another but supported and loved me until his death."

Mary's children were born to Cherokee fathers, Jim French (1872–1895) and Robert Lee Elliott (1872–1932). Mary, her husbands and children were born after the Civil War and never experienced slavery in the Cherokee Nation. Because Robert Elliott enrolled as Cherokee by blood, descendants of the Elliott children can still seek enrollment as Cherokee by blood through their father. The likelihood of slave owners creating children with slave women was real. The ability to prove it, however, was nil unless the father signed documents or gave testimony of paternity.

The existing Dawes roll cannot be changed. Freedmen listees were granted Cherokee citizenship by treaty. With Oklahoma statehood, the Cherokee Nation ended as a government. Decades later, it reorganized. Now only courts can decide if Freedmen descendants must be granted Cherokee citizenship rights if the Cherokee Nation's government rules otherwise. The Dawes era is over, but it casts a long shadow over the present. Today's new Cherokee citizens enroll by submitting certified birth certificates connecting themselves to Cherokee by blood enrollees.

Robert Elliott reported to the *Muskogee Times-Democrat* regarding his children after the trial, "I was told that it would make little difference how they were enrolled, as they were entitled to their land anyway." The main reason the Dawes Roll was established was to facilitate the allotment of

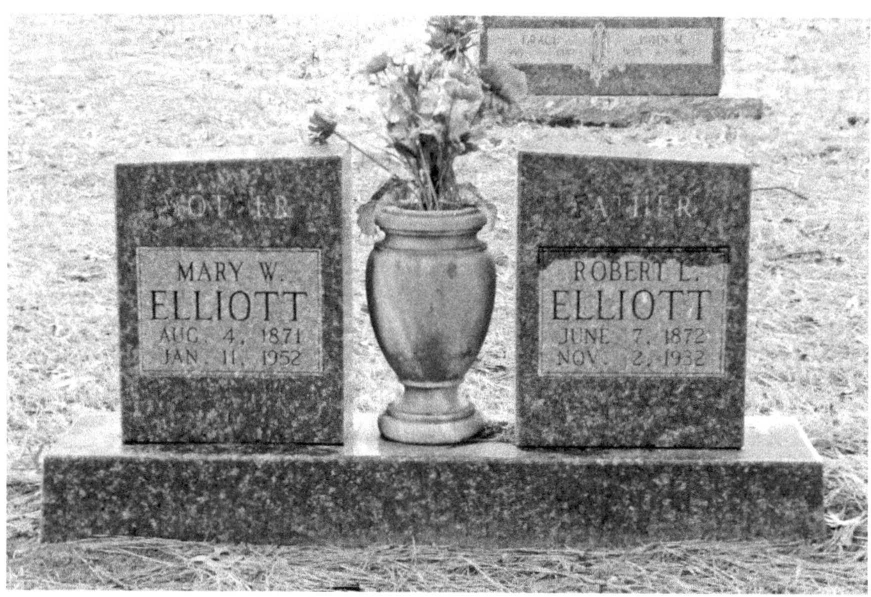

Mary and Robert Elliott's graves are at Memorial Park Cemetery in Muskogee. *Jim Roaix.*

communal Cherokee lands to its individuals. Both Freedmen and Cherokee citizens by blood would receive land, but Freedmen did receive smaller allotments. With the Cherokee Nation being superseded by the state, further benefits to being on the rolls were not expected. To the Elliotts, it didn't seem worth questioning—that is, until the school barred their children.

As to the outcome of the school case, the newspaper reported, "The six children of Mr. and Mrs. Robert Elliott are Indians with the blood of the redman and the Caucasian flowing through their veins, and are entitled to go to white schools." It is obvious that whites and Cherokees comprised the area's ruling society at that time. Nothing was lower than black. That attitude continued through KKK days, the Tulsa Race Riot, Jim Crow days and the Civil Rights Act integrating schools, and it continues with subtlety today.

Robert and Mary Elliott's children were Robert Lee (born in 1899), George Washington (born in 1901), William (born in 1904), Lometa (born in 1906), Ruth (born circa 1908) and Mary Jean (born circa 1920). The Elliotts were described in the newspaper as well-to-do farmers. The couple is buried at Memorial Park Cemetery in Muskogee. Mary died on January 11, 1952; Robert was born on June 7, 1872, in Canadian District and died in 1932. On the 1930 census, all their children still resided at home, seeming to refuse to leave the nest. The children then ranged in age from thirty down to twenty. Daughter Ruth married in 1930 after the census was taken. In 1940, her widowed mother, Mary Walker, was living in Muskogee with Ruth and her husband, Robert Douglas.

References

Ancestry.com, Fold 3, U.S. census, Dawes packets, Eastern Cherokee applications, family accounts, Find-a-Grave, cemetery sites and newspaper archives.

Hampton, David Keith. *Cherokee Mixed-Bloods.* Lincoln, AR: ARC Press of Cane Hill, 2005.

CHAPTER 18

CIVIL WAR VETERAN CORPORAL ALLEN LYNCH

Karen Coody Cooper

"My family is all Cherokee," reported Allen Lynch to Dawes Commissioners in May 1901 during his enrollment interview in Vinita, Indian Territory. His wife was Sarah Cynthia Clark (called Cynthia), born to Mary Ann Nave, the daughter of historic Cherokee chief John Ross's sister Annie Ross, who had married William Nave, a white man. Cynthia Clark was born on January 23, 1850, and she, along with her mother and sister, Emily, are recorded on the 1852 Drennen Roll.

Allen Lynch, born in January 1840, specifically gave notice to commissioners when he enrolled as a Freedman that his wife and resulting offspring were Cherokee by blood. But the white commissioners came from a world where one black ancestor overpowered the society value of seven white ancestors. During the process of Cherokee enrollment, the commissioners learned through experience that Cherokee Nation monitors would rarely intervene on behalf of black petitioners. No one was eager to enroll the children of black interviewees as Cherokee by blood.

The Lynches' quest to obtain Cherokee rights for their children would encompass ongoing battles requiring reams of paper, lawyer fees, notary payments, postal expenses and repeated interviews. There should have been one simple accurate enrollment with no expensive confusion to follow. However, the 1880 Cherokee Nation census had erroneously listed the couple and their five children as "Colored." Most people in the area were aware of the Clark girls being Cherokee members of the Ross family.

Census taker Joseph L. Thompson had fought for the Confederacy, but that is not necessarily what led to the error. The Lynch family and most other citizens would not have known what the census document reported about them until the Dawes Commission informed them twenty years after the census. The 1880 census became the document that refuted Lynch family entreaties. Corrections were promised vocally and in writing from time to time and then were reversed when officials viewed uncorrected copies of the 1880 records.

Through the Lynches' efforts, the 1880 official record was ultimately physically corrected by adding secondary notes handwritten in heavy bold ink with the citations "Mistake, Cherokee, not Colored" following on each of the lines listing Cynthia and her earliest children. There was no notation on that original document as to when it was corrected. However, countless uncorrected copies had already been distributed. When the Dawes Commission convened, corrected copies of the 1880 record were apparently not used during the fact-checking process. As late as July 1903, a commissioner wrote in response to Lynch son Andrew, "An examination of the authenticated tribal roll of 1880 for Delaware District show that the applicant's name is born thereon as Andrew Lynch, a colored person."

In February 1903, patriarch Allen Lynch appeared in person to appeal for corrections. The following exchange occurred:

Q. Your wife appears on the 1880 roll as a freedman?
A. No, she is Cherokee.
Q. She has no colored blood in her?
A. No, sir.
Q. She also appears on the 1896 roll as a freedman. How do you explain that?
A. I don't know.

It was obviously perplexing to Allen Lynch because in every interview, he and his family reiterated their situation, provided evidence and would be reassured that the family would be duly and correctly enrolled.

Cynthia was a seventh daughter of an unbroken Cherokee line (and to early Cherokee thinking, she would have been 100 percent Cherokee despite a preponderance of white blood through a succession of white men marrying her female ancestors). Her lineage traced back through Cherokee females all the way to Ghi-goo-ie, whose own mother was a Cherokee woman living in the mists of time when Cherokee life was seemingly true and constant. The line was an unbroken maternal line, in the old clan system practice, and made Cynthia more Cherokee than many of her cousins—and more than most of her contemporary acquaintances.

Allen mentioned during an interview that he had first been aware of Cynthia when she was a young child before the Civil War, when he was still a slave in the Delaware District of the Cherokee Nation. Cynthia's father, John Clark, abandoned his wife and two babies to go to California in search of gold and never returned (probably died), leaving his young family in embarrassing straits. Cynthia's mother married twice more, but both relationships ended in divorce. Cynthia and her siblings (expanded by two half siblings) likely experienced troubling childhoods, and then the war threw everything into havoc.

Mary took her children and fled to Kansas along with her slaves, who soon became free. Andy Frye, Mary's former slave, testified that he took Emily and Cynthia back to the Cherokee Nation at the end of the war, while their mother remained there until 1867, when Frye returned to Kansas to bring her back as well.

Allen had worked at a salt lick in the Cherokee Nation while serving as a slave of Joe Lynch, who owned a vast plantation and ferry. Becoming a

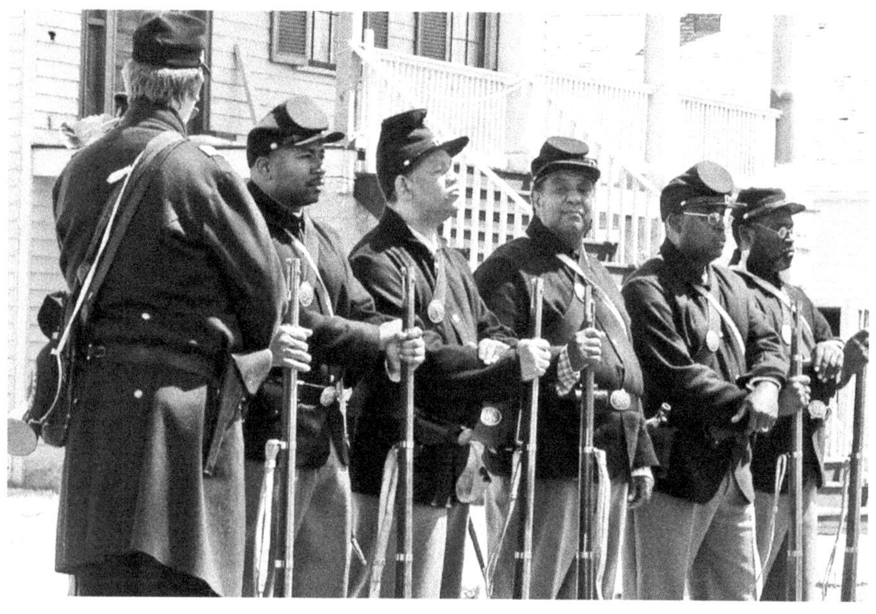

Reenactors at Fort Scott, Kansas, represent the First Kansas Colored Infantry, the first such regiment in the nation, formed on January 13, 1863. *Fort Scott National Historic Site.*

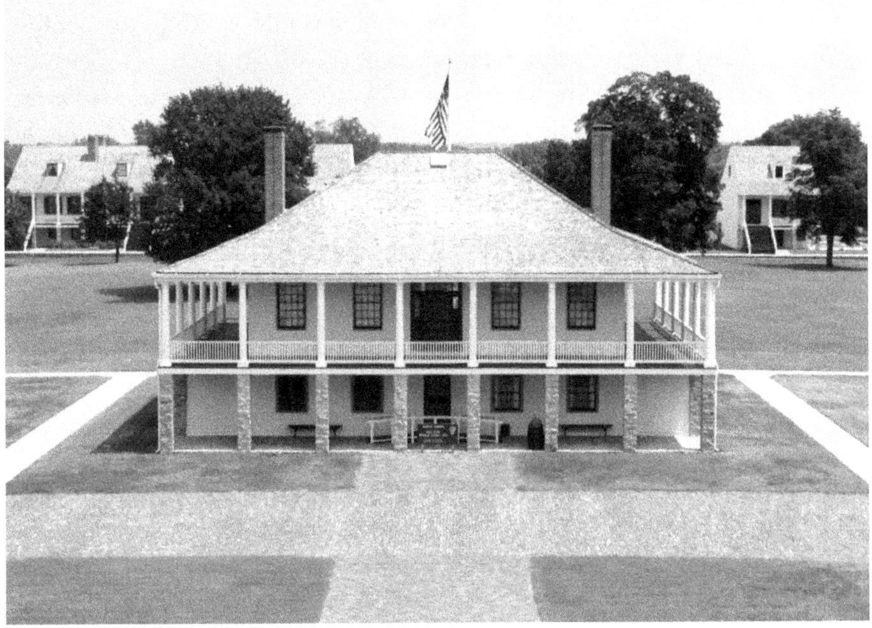

This hospital survived the Civil War at Fort Scott, Kansas, where Indian Territory refugees fled, with some joining the Union army. *Fort Scott National Historic Site.*

war refugee in Kansas, Allen signed up to protect the Union and became a corporal in the First Kansas Colored Infantry, which became the Seventy-Ninth United States Colored Troops, one of the last regiments to be mustered out at the end of the war on October 30, 1865. He fought at Cabin Creek and received an injury at Honey Springs. He apparently was literate despite laws forbidding the education of slaves. Cynthia became a teacher following the war. Perhaps Cynthia taught Allen to read and write. The couple married in the fall of 1867 and produced five sons (one dying as an infant) and four daughters. Allen apparently became a successful farmer in a time when children provided valuable labor and individuals could fence as much land as they would put into production.

In 1883, Cynthia and her six eldest children can be found duly recorded on a Cherokee by blood list for receiving a per capita distribution. In 1904, the acting Secretary of the Interior sent the Dawes Commission a two-and-a-half-page letter detailing the occurrence of errors regarding the Lynch family and dictating that Cynthia Lynch was to be enrolled as a citizen by blood and that her children were entitled to the same treatment. This letter possibly resulted in the physical corrections made to the 1880 Cherokee census record, but extant uncorrected copies would continue to confuse those who used the census as a reference.

The eldest son, Edward B. Lynch, was born in 1871. He sat before the commissioners in Vinita on September 29, 1900, reported that he was one-eighth Cherokee and named his parents. The file report notes that he was approved for enrollment as Cherokee by blood. However, on February 2, 1904, a letter to Edward states that the commission decided on September 18, 1903, that certain children of Cynthia had been enrolled as Freedmen and that the Cherokee Nation had not protested the classification, although Cynthia had protested. The letter states that the commission on November 9, 1903, decided to approve those children, and if the secretary approved the change, then Edward could request his classification be changed to Cherokee by blood if he so desired.

On March 4, 1904, the commission sent the Secretary of the Interior a four-page letter reiterating the errors made regarding Cynthia and her children and noted, "Under the facts stated these children are quarter blood Cherokee Indians." It seemed everyone understood that the children should be enrolled as Cherokee by blood, but had all the adult Lynch children been duly advised that they must again take action to be removed from the Freedman list and placed onto the Cherokee by blood roll? Additionally, adult grandchildren would have needed to take action because the Dawes Commission and the Cherokee Nation absented themselves from correcting their own errors.

On August 12, 1904, son Edward sent his letter to request enrollment as Cherokee by blood. The letter is on letterhead stationery (of lawyer William H. Vann). On August 25, an order was issued to the Department of the Interior that Edward be listed as Cherokee by blood. It was so ordered by the commission on April 24, 1905. On July 27, 1905, a new corrected Dawes enrollment sheet was drawn up for Edward, and his previous erroneous one was stamped "Cancelled."

Edward's brother Andrew mailed a short letter to Vinita commissioners on March 17, 1906: "I, Andrew Lynch hereby empower and employ E.H. Smith as my attorney to look after my business of getting my enrollment transferred from the Cherokee Freedmen rolls to the Cherokee rolls."

Andrew received a ten-page letter of babble-speak saying that since he and his sister Mary Kelley each accepted the land allotments offered to them, they had therefore accepted being enrolled as Freedmen. A letter dated April 1, 1907, told Andrew, "You are hereby advised that the application for the transfer of your name from the roll of Cherokee freedman to the roll of Cherokees by blood, was denied by the Secretary of the Interior, March 4, 1907." Statehood came; the rolls closed.

Mary Kelley's Cherokee Nation citizens enrollment form was also stamped "CANCELLED." A folder for "Cherokee 3631 Mary E. Kelley" cited, "Transferred to Cherokee Freedman 1257." A pristine new Freedmen form is on file duly notated with stamps and dates of the steps taken. Mary's four-year-old daughter is listed with her.

Allen's brother Anderson Lynch, also a Freedman, married Cynthia's half sister, Ruth Downing. Ruth enrolled herself and her children, and her family endured similar challenges requiring repeated interviews. At one point, Ruth was noted as an "adopted colored," even though she and others reported that she was Cherokee, and she admitted that she and her husband were living separately. Cynthia's full sister Emily Jane married Willis Battles, apparently a white man noted as "citizen by intermarriage" after having married Emily, who is duly recorded as a Cherokee citizen. Her interview reveals her struggles to make a living after the Civil War, relying on relatives, friends, boyfriends and, most of all, the former slave of her mother, Andy Frye and his wife, who were the most constant assistants during Emily's indigent life of hardship and sickness. Skin color as a barrier made no sense to these Cherokee sisters or to the former Cherokee slaves who knew them.

Cynthia Clark Lynch died on September 10, 1908, and is buried at Ketchum Cemetery in Craig County. Her tombstone is large, topped with a carving of the Bible. She is noted as the wife of Allen Lynch, and the marker reads, "In remembrance of our darling mother." Nearby is a modest marker for their unnamed infant son. The parents are noted on that stone as "A. & Synthia Lynch."

Second son Bert William Lynch was born on March 1, 1873. The government struggled to term him black, while his parents fought to record him as Cherokee, but Bert moved to California and foiled them all by becoming white. The 1930 census reports him to be white, working as a foreman earning a salary on a farm in Imperial, California. When he obtained his Social Security number in 1937, the administration recorded Bert as white and listed his parents as Allen Lynch and Cynthia Clark. The 1940 census noted him as white, living on a pension in Oakland. His education level was noted as seventh grade. He died in December 1940 and is buried at Cypress Lawn Memorial Park in San Mateo County, California.

Patriarch Allen Lynch inspired people with his memories of being a soldier in the Civil War. Jess C. Epple was a young man when elder veteran Lynch began talking about his experiences at nearby Honey Springs battlefield,

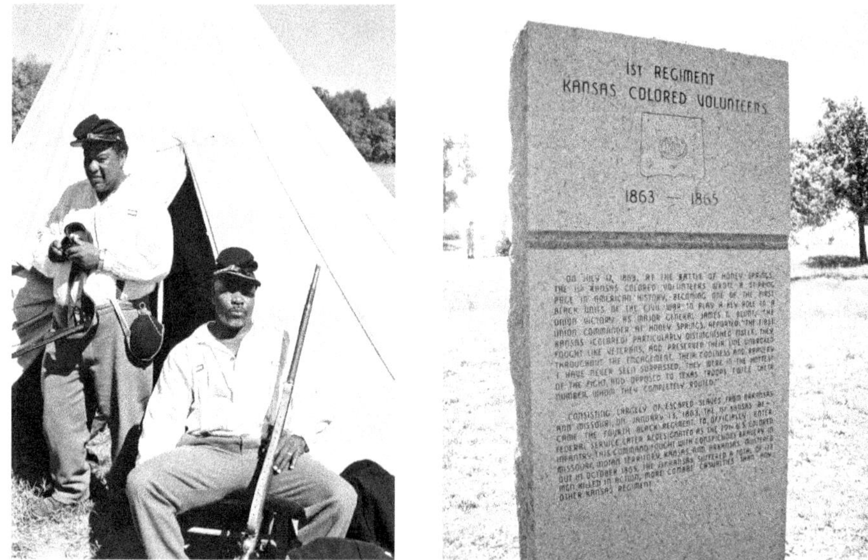

Left: Reenactors represent the First Kansas Colored Infantry at the Battle of Honey Springs near present-day Rentiesville, Oklahoma. *Oklahoma Historical Society*.

Right: Monuments at the Honey Springs battle site honor the heroism of the First Kansas Colored Infantry. *Oklahoma Historical Society*.

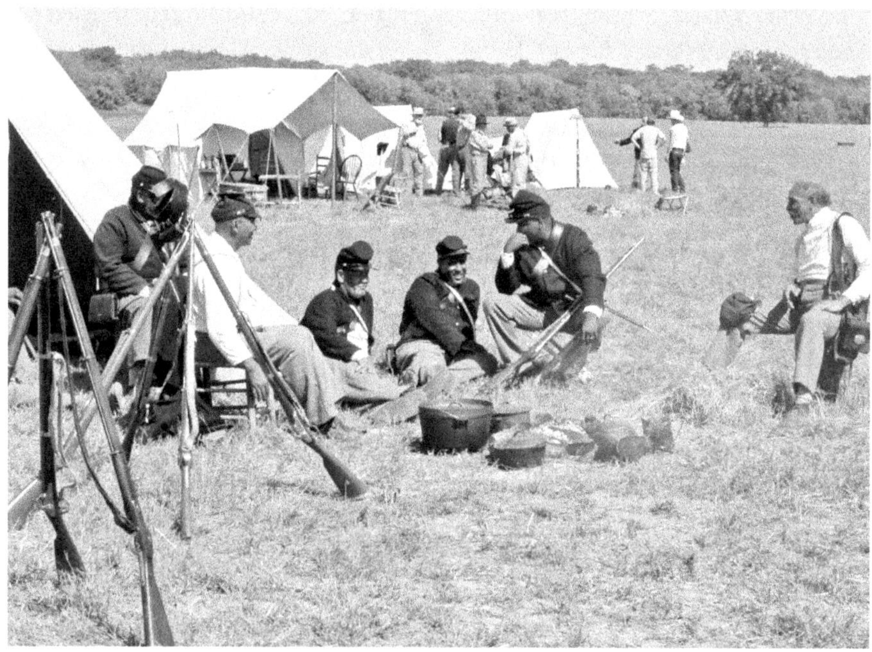

Volunteers reenact the infantry encamped at Honey Springs. *Oklahoma Historical Society*.

leading Epple to gain an interest in Civil War history. Epple's son explained, "Lynch was always welcome at my Grandparents....My Father and Lynch begin this long process about the time the Tulsa Race Riots were happening."

Allen had been mustered into the army at Fort Scott, Kansas, on January 26, 1863, as a private in the First Kansas Colored Infantry and mustered out as a corporal of the Seventy-Ninth US Colored Infantry on October 1, 1865, at Pine Bluffs, Arkansas.

Major General James G. Blunt's report following the battle at Honey Springs Depot, near Rentiesville, sets the scene: "I immediately commenced crossing my forces at the mouth of Grand River in boats, and, by 10 p.m. of the 16th [of July 1863], commenced moving south, with less than 3,000 men, mostly Indians and negroes, and twelve pieces of artillery."

As he finished describing the decisive battle, he wrote, "The First Kansas (colored) particularly distinguished itself; they fought like veterans, and preserved their line unbroken throughout the engagement. Their coolness and bravery I have never seen surpassed...they were in the hottest of the fight, and opposed to Texas troops twice their number, whom they completely routed. One Texas regiment that fought against them went into the fight with 300 men and came out with only 60. It would be invidious to make particular mention of any one where all did their duty so well."

Allen's records had most often reported his birthdate as 1840, but the 1920 census reported him living in Beck, McIntosh County, at the age of eighty-two, giving him a birthdate of 1838. In 1930, his birthdate is noted as 1833, based on Lynch reporting his age to be ninety-seven and residing in the boardinghouse of Sinia Fulson in Beck. Allen died on May 27, 1933, having reportedly attained the age of one hundred, and Fulson ordered a veteran's headstone on March 12, 1934, to be delivered to the rail station in Muskogee and engraved locally. Allen was interred at Nancy Shepherd Cemetery in Warner. Nancy Shepherd was Allen's sister.

References

Dawes Commission records, Fold 3 and ancestry.com.

Epple, Jess C. *Honey Springs Depot*. N.p.: self-published, 1964. Revised in 2002 by Jess C. Epple Jr., who renewed the copyright.

CHAPTER 19

LEE STREET MEMORIES

GROWING UP ON DEPOT HILL

Ty Wilson

I was born in Tahlequah, Oklahoma, on June 19, 1971. I lived most of my childhood at 500 South Lee Avenue, Tahlequah, with my grandmother Minerva Wilson. Lee Avenue was the main street in the last predominantly black Cherokee neighborhood in the capital city of the Cherokee Nation. I remember as a child in the '70s the elders of the neighborhood did not discuss being Cherokee very much. We were only told that we were Cherokee and couldn't prove it. Yet I grew up knowing that I have Indian blood the same way I knew I had African blood and European blood. I had relatives who looked Indian. I had relatives who looked African. I had relatives who looked white. Yet we were all from the same family.

When I grew up in the neighborhood in the '70s, it was filled with several different families. Although we were not all kin, the community functioned as one cohesive family. Everyone helped one another out. Everyone helped with one another's kids. Everyone helped the elders. If I was playing at someone's house when it was dinnertime, I ate with them. If I got into trouble at someone else's house, their parent would spank me and send me home to tell my grandmother what I did. There were no strangers in the neighborhood. Everyone knew one another. Even though everyone did not get along within our community, when confronted with an outsider, everyone showed a united front.

In the '70s, that neighborhood was self-sustaining. Starting from the north on Mission Street, we had Antioch Baptist Church. West of the

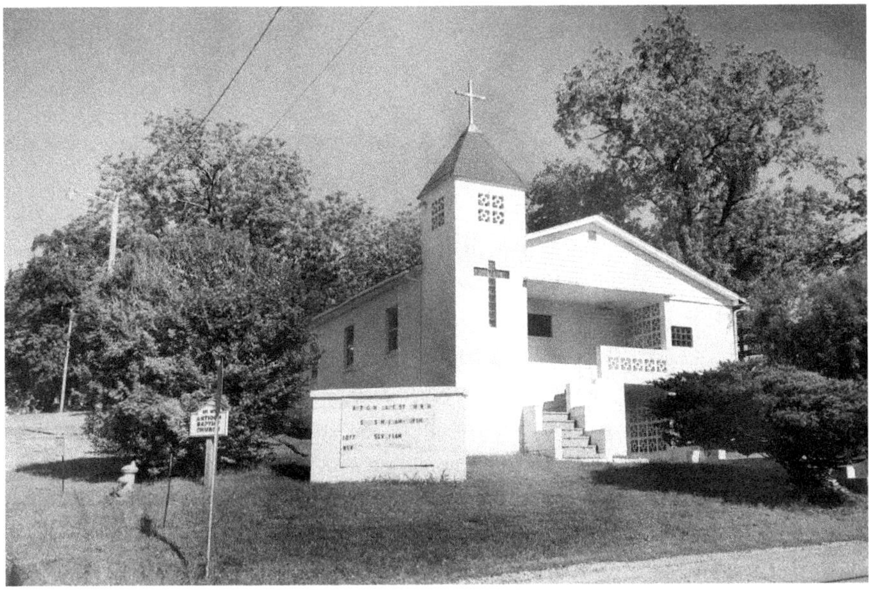

The old Antioch Baptist Church was established in 1877 in Tahlequah, was remodeled several times and survived a firebombing in 1997. *Ty Wilson.*

church on the land of the old train depot, we had Lee Street Park, which consisted of an outdoor basketball court next to the Old Depot, a softball field with a stand for spectators, as well as swings, a merry-go-round and a teeter totter. Out of the park, going straight, we had a pool hall on one side of the street and a grocery store on the other side. On farther down the street there was a nightclub.

As a child, like every other child in the neighborhood, I went to Antioch Church. Not all adults went to church, but even those who did not go to church would still put cash in the offering. The pastor and deacons would go all around the neighborhood visiting and collecting the offering. At Christmastime, it didn't matter if your family went to church or not—the church members would bring a bag of candy and fruit to everyone in the neighborhood. The church played a vital part in keeping the community together. The park was another neighborhood gathering spot. Every summer there would be fast-pitch softball tournaments for adults. Several guys from the neighborhood had their own team, named the Malibus. My summers were filled with things to do. My grandfather would take me fishing and picking wild onions and watercress. In the wintertime, my grandfather would take us hunting and to cut trees that we used for heat.

When we were in the forest, he would point out different plants that they would use for medicine when he was growing up. I was raised to respect adults and especially my elders.

The neighborhood was so close that even when people began moving away and leaving homes empty, those of us still living there would keep their grass cut and their yards clean. We were taught an exceptional work ethic by our elders. That included some tough life lessons centered on perceptions and judgment coming from other people. Those lessons prepared me for the world around me and helped me through many obstacles I have encountered as an adult. I try to instill those same principles in my children. The difference is that they don't have the support system of a viable, close-knit community the way I did as a child. I can only share with them my stories and the feeling that comes from true security in the midst of a very uncertain world. Families have been forced to move away, and there isn't much left of the neighborhood. Some of the older kids can remember a little, but for the younger ones, they have no idea of the sanctuary we all shared in those times. It saddens me to think of that era being merely a memory. That is why I will do everything in my power to restore our once thriving Cherokee community. I will do all I can to ensure that the future generations to come will have at least a taste of what we were so fortunate to have growing up.

I want to wrap this up with a few thoughts about my grandmother. I say "wrap up" instead of "end" because this is not the end of my story. Minerva Wilson was an amazing lady. She was strong yet loving. She could put you in your place, but the whole time you knew how much she loved you. There was never a hungry mouth at her house. Sometimes I felt like she took one chicken and divided into one hundred pieces, and everyone got full. I don't know how she did it, but she could stretch a dollar and a meal to make sure we all had plenty. Everyone knew they were welcome in her home, and if she had it, we had it. She was the foundation of our home, family and community. She was my grandma, and she still lives in all of us. It is our job to restore what she and others worked so hard to give us. I want all future generations to know that sense of belonging that is so dear to my heart. I want them to know how it feels to truly be home.

APPENDIX I

BLACK CEMETERIES IN THE CHEROKEE NATION

There are tragic "lost cemetery" stories concerning numerous black cemeteries, now unmarked; headstones thrown in streams; graves plowed over and more. There are also stories of generosity displayed in times of rampant segregation. One such tale concerns Sanders Cemetery in Nowata County. Reportedly, a family of white pioneers was crossing the open lands near the black town of Sanders and died of typhoid. Cemeteries at that time were segregated, so the pastor of the black church decided to turn the property in front of the church into a "white" cemetery and saw to it that the family was given their last rites there.

As for lost cemeteries, the largest and oldest might be an unnamed cemetery for slaves at Park Hill. At some time, all markers were removed (perhaps most had been decayed wood, but some memories report that stones were tossed in the river), and a wall foundation is evident (while all signs of previous fencing above ground is gone). It was said to have been a cemetery for slaves of the area, Park Hill having been generally a wealthy neighborhood. The property is currently owned by the Cherokee Nation and was tested with ground-penetrating radar revealing burials and the foundation surrounding the cemetery.

The following information on black cemeteries has been gleaned from various sources but has not been verified through visits to sites. There are more lost cemeteries yet to be noted. There should be many slave burials in the Webbers Falls area and near other former homes of the largest Cherokee slaveholders in other areas of the Cherokee Nation. A few of the following

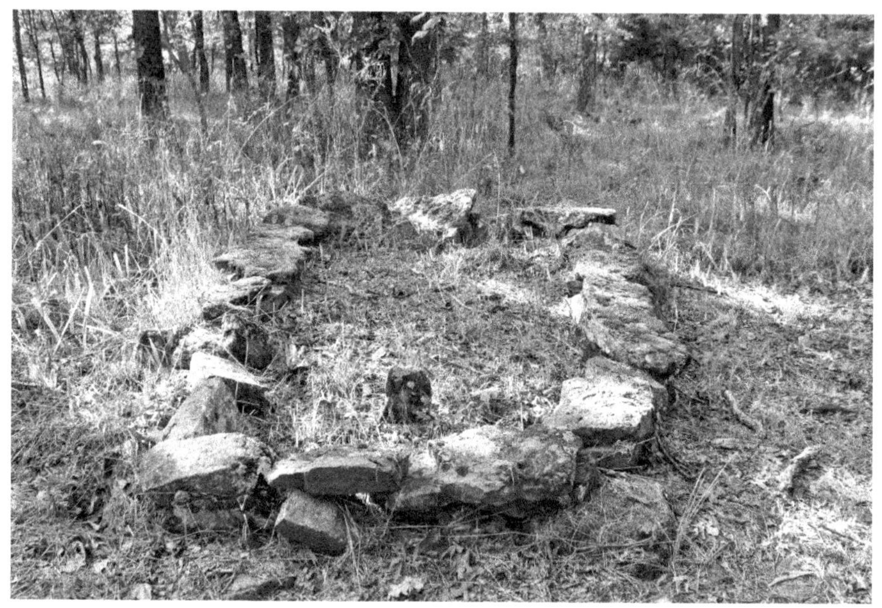

This page: Unmarked graves and a broken headstone, as seen at the Alberty Family Cemetery, are not unusual in old, remote graveyards. *Mark A. Harrison.*

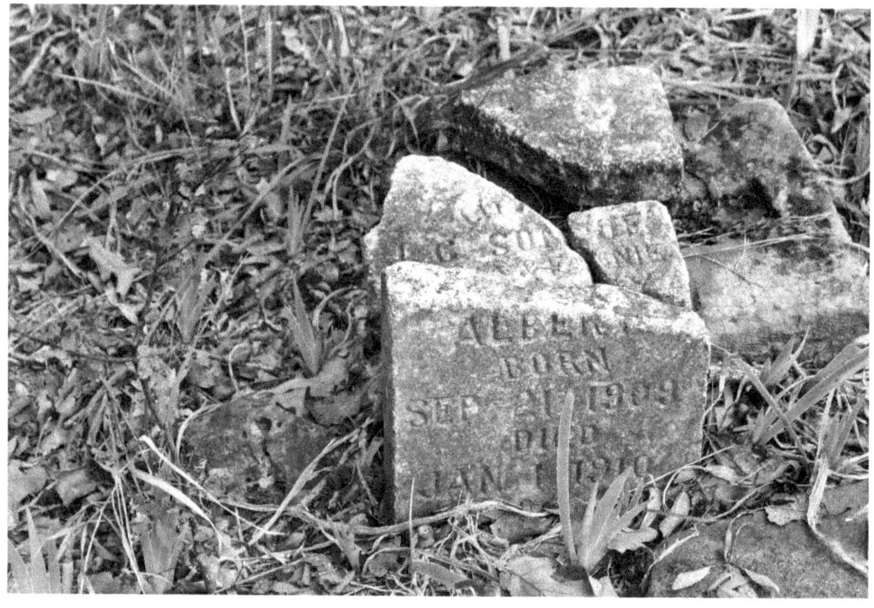

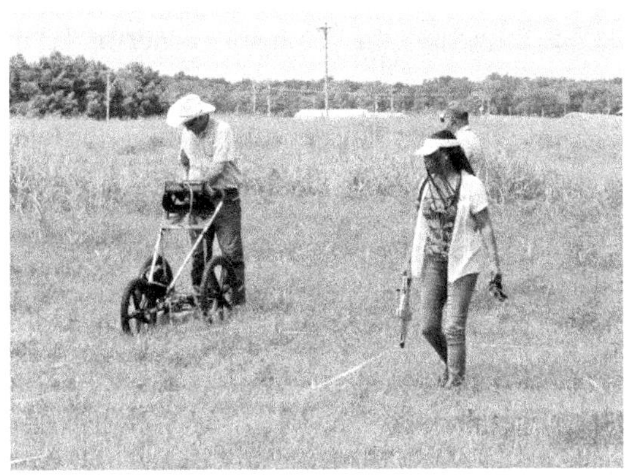

Ian Garrison with his father, Erv Garrison, behind Rodslen Brown, work with penetrating radar to locate unmarked graves in old slave cemetery at Park Hill. *Will Chavez, from the* Cherokee Phoenix.

cemeteries are integrated cemeteries containing a noted black burial. The first cemetery in the following list happens to be within the confines of Camp Walahili, managed by Camp Fire Organization. Many years ago, a young girl wrote the following poem while attending the camp, and for years afterward, campers would learn and recite the poem when visiting the cemetery:

"Poor Old Slave"

The poor old slave
Has gone to rest
We know that he is free
His bones they lie
Disturb them not
Way down at Waluhili.

ALBERTY FAMILY CEMETERY, Chouteau, Wagoner County, includes eight marked interments and numerous unmarked graves. Former Cherokee councilman Jerry Alberty is buried here. The Camp Fire Organization has owned the surrounding property since 1949. To access the cemetery, contact camp administrators at 918-592-2267.

BECK CEMETERY, in the Tuxedo area on Cook Creek, Washington County, is named for Sam Beck and was started by Doc Tann, two prominent black men in the area.

BOOKER T. WASHINGTON CEMETERY is located at the southeast corner of Fern Mountain Road and U.S. Highway 69, in Muskogee (outside the Cherokee Nation). It is a large cemetery. George F. Nave is buried there.

CENTER POINT CEMETERY is located about one mile north of Redland in Sequoyah County. Entry is on the south side of State Highway 101.

FORT GIBSON CITIZENS CEMETERY (also known as Cherokee National Cemetery) is one and a half miles east of Fort Gibson. Begun in the 1850s, it contains several graves of note, including for Reverend Frank Vann and the deadly outlaw Cherokee Bill.

FOUR MILE BRANCH BAPTIST CHURCH CEMETERY is located four miles east of Fort Gibson and one mile north of Highway 62 on Four Mile Stop Road (first road one quarter mile north of church). It was founded in 1867.

GOOSE NECK BEND CEMETERY is east of Lenapah on Goose Neck Bend of the Verdigris River.

HICKORY CREEK CEMETERY is two miles north of Lenapah on Highway 169. To access it, you must go east on EW8 and turn south on the gravel road Little Flock Road. The Little Flock Church is on the west side of the gravel road. The cemetery was begun in the 1860s.

JACKSON CEMETERY, Section 8, R15E, T17N, Shahan Township, Wagoner County, is one quarter mile from Jackson Grove Cemetery.

JACKSON GROVE CEMETERY is one quarter mile off 141st on Jackson Grove Road (225th East Avenue), next to Jackson Grove Baptist Church, Shahan Township, Wagoner County. It appears to have been started in the 1920s.

LYNCH PRAIRIE CEMETERY was begun as a Freedman burial site. It is not fenced, but it contained ninety-eight burials. It is also known as Island Ford Cemetery. It is in Mayes County, Section 29, R21E, T23N.

MADDEN CEMETERY, or Salt Creek Cemetery, is in Nowata County (noted in the Oakley-Schofield book).

MANLEY-ROSS CEMETERY is in Craig County (noted in the Oakley-Schofield book).

NANCY SHEPHERD CEMETERY is in Warner. Take Highway 64 north for three miles, turn left onto 153 Street (gravel) and go two miles, crossing a low water bridge, with the cemetery just after it.

PANTHER CREEK CEMETERY is in Rogers County (noted in the Oakley-Schofield book).

ROSE LAWN CEMETERY is near the southern edge of the city of Vian in Section 27, Township 12 North, Range 22 East in Sequoyah County. It had been known as Vian Colored Cemetery. Many of the graves there were relocated from Sandtown Cemetery, which had been three miles northwest of Tamaha, in Section 7, Township 11 North, Range 22 East.

ROSS CEMETERY is on Bliss Avenue in Tahlequah directly across from W.W. Hastings Hospital. The cemetery was purchased by Stick Ross to preserve it.

SALT CREEK CEMETERY, or Madden Cemetery, is in Nowata County (noted in the Oakley-Schofield book).

SANDERS CEMETERY is in Nowata County (noted in the Oakley-Schofield book).

SANDTOWN CEMETERY—see Rose Lawn Cemetery.

SHADY GROVE CEMETERY is in the Pryor Creek Community, Rogers County (noted in the Oakley-Schofield book).

TUCKER CEMETERY is in Craig County (noted in the Oakley-Schofield book).

VIAN COLORED CEMETERY—see Rose Lawn Cemetery.

References

Find-a-Grave website.

Nowata County OKGenWeb online post.

Oakley, Mary May, and Constance Ann Schofield. *Six Freedmen Cemeteries: Tucker, Sanders, Salt Creek, Panther Creek, Manley-Ross and Shady Grove (Nowata, Craig and Rogers Counties)*. Vinita, OK, 2005.

APPENDIX II

HISTORIC BLACK BAPTIST CHURCHES

Joe Wilson and Karen Coody Cooper

ANTIOCH BAPTIST CHURCH, 320 South Mission Avenue, Tahlequah, was established in 1877 by Reverend Daniel Rogers, who was sent to this area by the American Baptist Mission Board of New York. He created a white church and a black church and was a circuit preacher. The building for the black congregation was dedicated in 1879. Baptisms were held at the Village Springs Stream, property now owned by Northeastern State University. A WPA interview in 1938 finds Cornelius Neely Nave, born in 1868, recalling that his slave father had been born "just about where the colored church stands on Depot Hill." His slave cabin, owned by Daniel Nave (son of a sister of John Ross), was where the church was built.

Reverend Teamer oversaw a rebuilding of the structure in 1906, and Reverend P.D. Davis oversaw another refurbishment in 1962. In 1997, on the eve of Martin Luther King Day, the church was firebombed. News coverage at that time said the white brick building had been erected 34 years before and that the location had been used for the church for 119 years before the firebombing. Damage was about $1,000, and repairs were made. Reverend Walter Brown was pastor at the time, retiring in 2000 after serving for 18 years.

The church building closed in 2016 when the pastor moved the congregation to a larger facility on the other side of Tahlequah, selling the old neighborhood facility.

EBENEZER BAPTIST CHURCH was founded in Melvin, a post office site from 1894 to 1919, along the Tahlequah–Wagoner Road, west of present-day Hulbert. The town appears on an 1896 map along with the name of Zack Taylor, who owned the store that provided the post office. He was killed when his store was robbed, and the town evolved into a primarily black settlement. A 1948 topographical map shows a church, a school, about a dozen houses, an abandoned railroad line and the soon-to-be-impounded Fort Gibson Lake. This map indicates that the church was being used as a school at the time.

FIRST BAPTIST CHURCH, Fort Gibson, was organized and built as a log cabin on the corner of Lee and Hickory Streets in 1869. A one-room structure, it was lit with kerosene lamps hung on the walls. Old-fashioned wood benches provided seating for adults, while children sat on the floor in front of the pulpit. A big potbellied stove sat in the middle of the church. In 1920, a new building was provided across the street and deeded in the name of First Baptist Church (Colored). When the Lincoln School burned in 1949 or 1950, the church served as the school location until the school was rebuilt. Baptisms occurred in a pond behind Garrison Hill and later at Grand River. A baptistery was completed in 1954 during the pastoring of Reverend P.D. Davis. In 2001, the congregation voted to change the name of the church to Historic First Baptist Church.

FOUNTAIN BAPTIST CHURCH, the oldest continuing church congregation in Oklahoma, was founded on September 9, 1832, in Haynes, a postal site from January 1904 through May 1914, five miles north of Muskogee in Wagoner County. The first pastor was Reverend John Davis, succeeded by Reverend David Rollins. In the 1860s and '70s, it also served as the school for the surrounding community. In 1933, Reverend J.C. Wade became the pastor, paid fifty cents a week. The church provided a meeting place for representatives of Creek freedmen to plan meetings with the federal BIA regarding inclusion in the Creek Nation. The church building was rebuilt in 1956 when Reverend S.W. Woodfork was pastor, and it was at that time affiliated with the Masonic Prince Hall Trinity Lodge No. 84.

FOUR MILE BAPTIST CHURCH was established at the end of the Civil War after Freedmen began congregating at Fort Gibson and a cholera epidemic led to Cherokee Nation efforts to disperse the overcrowded conditions with partial resettlement away from Fort Gibson, four miles distant. Thus, the Four Mile Baptist Church was formalized in 1867 by Reverend Samuel Solomon.

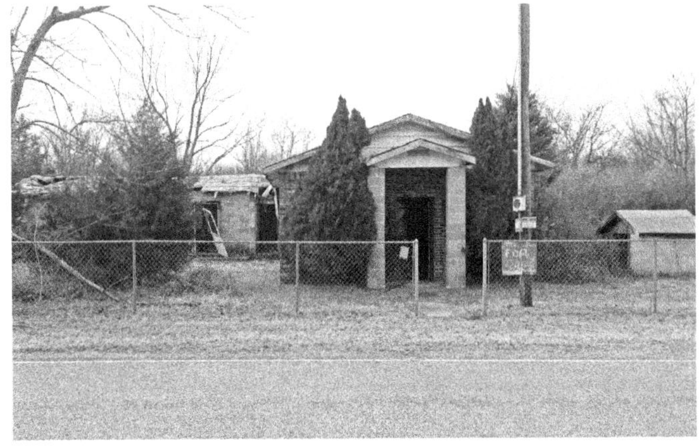

Ebenezer Baptist Church in Melvin, a former town, also served as a school, but it is derelict now. *Ty Wilson.*

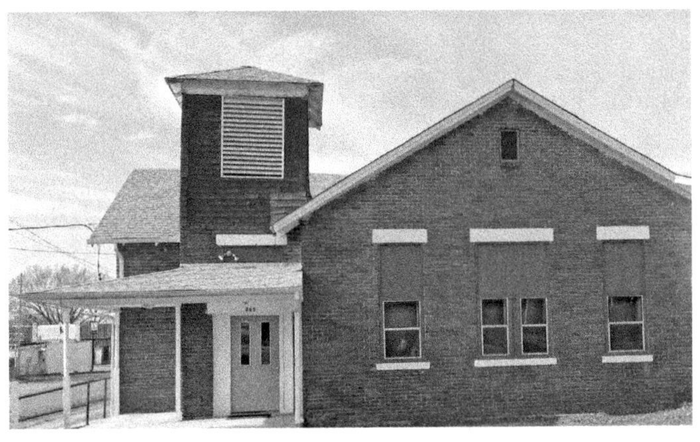

The Historic First Baptist Church of Fort Gibson was founded in 1860 in a log structure and was rebuilt across the street in 1920. *Ty Wilson.*

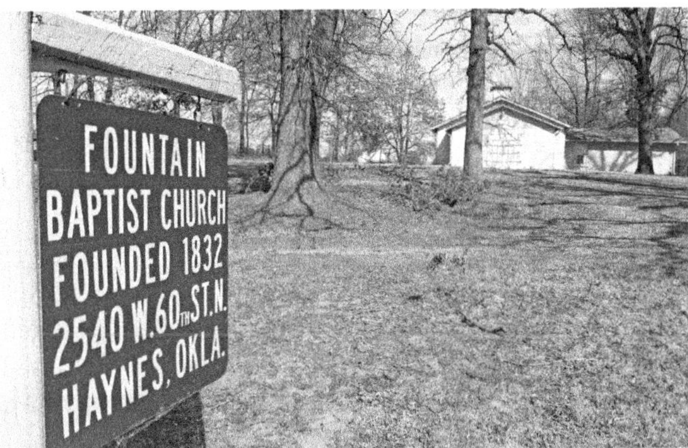

The Fountain Baptist Church may be the oldest church in Oklahoma, having been founded in 1832 in Haynes. It aided Creek Indians during the allotment era and was affiliated with the Mason's Prince Hall fellowship. *Ty Wilson.*

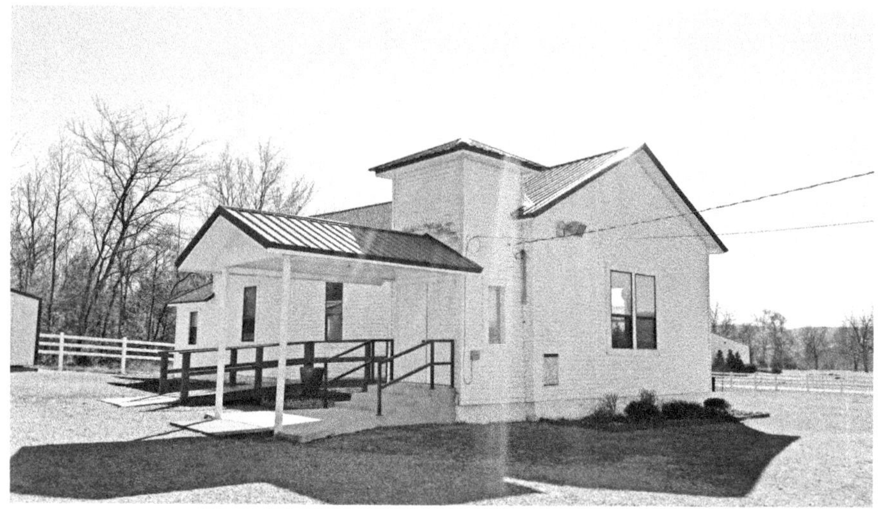

The Four Mile Baptist Church was organized in 1867 after a cholera outbreak at Fort Gibson led to a resettlement four miles away. *Ty Wilson.*

HICKORY CREEK CHURCH/LITTLE FLOCK BAPTIST CHURCH and Colored School began in Nowata County in the late 1870s. The first building was a log cabin on the south side of Hickory Creek. Five women took in washing to pay the expenses of building the school, which also served as a church. When flooding occurred, the traveling preacher couldn't get to the church, so the women raised additional money to build another log cabin on the other side of the creek. Services were conducted on Saturdays since the preacher came from Coffeyville, where he preached on Sundays. The preacher referred to the women as his "little flock," and he began calling the church the Little Flock Baptist Church. There is a historical marker at the location. A new church was built in the 1940s after one of the churches burned down. The county leased the land for the church for ninety-nine years after the land was lost when no one could pay the taxes back in the 1930s. Little Flock Road runs in front of the church.

This list is not complete. Much history has been lost, or only fragments of memories remain. Small communities struggled to form and rebuild their lives following the Civil War. Statehood and allotment often caused relocations, followed by the Dust Bowl and the Depression, from which the area was slow to recover. Preachers were often laymen and unpaid, yet churches were generally major cornerstones of community interactions.

APPENDIX III

RACE DEMOGRAPHICS IN CHEROKEE NATION

When original Cherokee hegemony was threatened by white intrusions in the eighteenth century, Cherokee populations reacted hostilely. As whites intermarried, their ability to effectively deal with outside white entities helped place white Cherokees in leadership positions. The move to Indian Territory and then the Civil War led to large losses of Cherokee life. As statehood loomed, outside whites sought to sublimate Native populations in Oklahoma. In the early part of the twentieth century, American Indians typically faced economic struggles and were relegated to a powerless existence. Allotment and Oklahoma statehood reduced most individually accrued Cherokee wealth and shelved the Cherokee government for decades to come. Economic success via federally allowed casino operations returned power and wealth to the Cherokee. The current growth of ethnic populations in Oklahoma serves to reduce white hegemony. If all minorities formed a coalition, they would have a political voice of strength, but minorities are not necessarily cohesive with other minority groups, so they are unlikely to act as a bloc. Census records become harder to discern and analyze regarding race as people become more genetically complex. The game of numbers can reveal or obfuscate reality, and different scholars have drawn different conclusions when searching through early population numbers.

Appendix III

1835 Cherokee Numbers Before Removal

Cherokee citizens	16,543
slaves	1,592

From Daniel Littlefield.

1860 Cherokee Nation Census—Before Civil War

Cherokee citizens	85%	18,773
slaves	11%	2,511
whites	3%	716
Total	**100%**	**22,000**

Based on Russell Thornton study.

1880 Cherokee Nation Census—After Reconstruction

Cherokee citizens	67%	15,307
adopted whites	20%	4,585
blacks	12%	2,777
Total	**100%**	**22,667**

From Katja May study.

1890 U.S. Census in Cherokee Nation—Outsiders Flood In

whites	51%	29,166
Cherokee	39%	22,015
blacks	9%	5,127
Total	**100%**	**56,308**

From Katja May study.

Appendix III

1900 U.S. Census in Cherokee Nation—Outsiders Grow, Indian Identity Diminishes

whites	66%	66,951
Indians	25%	25,639
blacks	9%	9,162
Total	**100%**	**101,752**

From Katja May study.

Oklahoma Demographics during Forty Years

Oklahoma	1970	1990	2000	2010
white	89.1%	82.1%	76.2%	72.2%
Native	3.8%	8.0%	7.9%	8.6%
black	6.7%	7.4%	7.6%	7.4%
Asian	0.1%	1.1%	1.4%	1.7%
Islander	---	---	0.1%	0.1%
other	0.2%	1.3%	2.4%	4.1%
two or more races	---	---	4.5%	5.9%

From en.wikipedia.org/wiki/Oklahoma.

2000 U.S. Census of Cherokee County, Oklahoma

white	56%	23,985
American Indian	32%	13,787
black	1%	509
Hispanic	4%	1,760
two races and others	6%	2,480
Total	**100%**	**42,521**

From U.S. census bureau data.

Appendix III

Tahlequah Oklahoma, based on 2010 Census

white alone	46.4%
American Indian alone	29.2%
two or more races	12.6%
Hispanic	10.0%
Asian alone	0.3%
other race alone	0.05%

From www.city-data.com/city/Tahlequah-Oklahoma.html.

READING LIST

Abel, Annie H. *The American Indian as Slaveholder and Secessionist.* Cleveland, OH, 1915.

African American & African Ancestored Genealogy. www.afrigeneas.com.

Burton, Art T. *Black, Red and Deadly: Black and Indian Gunfighters of Indian Territory.* Woodway, TX: Eakin Press, 1991.

Debo, Angie. *And Still the Waters Run: The Betrayal of the Five Civilized Tribes.* Princeton, NJ: Princeton University Press, 1940. Reprint, Norman: University of Oklahoma Press, 1984.

Halliburton, R., Jr. *Red Over Black: Black Slavery Among the Cherokee Indians.* Westport, CT, 1977.

Littlefield, Daniel F. *The Cherokee Freedmen: From Emancipation to American Citizenship.* Westport, CT: Greenwood Press, 1978.

May, Katja. *African Americans and Native Americans in the Creek and Cherokee Nations, 1830s to 1920s: Collision and Collusion.* New York: Garland Publishing, 1996.

Miles, Tiya. *The House on Diamond Hill: A Cherokee Plantation Story.* Chapel Hill: University of North Carolina Press, 2010.

———. *Ties that Bind: The Story of an Afro-Cherokee Family in Slavery and Freedom.* Berkeley: University of California Press, 2005.

Naylor, Celia E. *African Cherokees in Indian Territory: From Chattel to Citizens.* Chapel Hill: University of North Carolina Press, 2008.

Perdue, Theda. *Slavery and the Evolution of Cherokee Society, 1540–1866.* Knoxville: University of Tennessee Press, 1979.

Sturm, Circe. *Blood Politics: Race, Culture, and Identity in the Cherokee Nation of Oklahoma.* Berkeley: University of California Press, 2002.
Walton-Raji, Angela Y. African-nativeamerican.blogspot.com.
Who Is Nicka Smith? www.whoisnickasmith.com.

In editors T. Lindsay Baker and Julie P. Baker's *WPA Oklahoma Slave Narratives* (Norman: University of Oklahoma Press, 1996), the following Cherokee-related narratives (slave owner in parentheses) can be found:

p. 44: Bean, Joe (Dick Bean)
p. 48: Bean, Nancy (Rogers)
p. 194: Henderson, Henry (Vann)
p. 274: McNair, Chaney (William Penn Adair)
p. 301: Nave, Cornelius (Neely) (Naves and Vanns)
p. 314: Perryman, Patsy (surname of a Creek husband; Taylor)
p. 316: Petite/Petit, Phyllis (Thompson and Harnage)
p. 247: Richardson, Chaney (Charles Rogers, then Hannah Ross)
p. 355: Robertson, Betty/Belle Roberson (Vann)
p. 364: Rowe, Katie (her husband had been with Rowe)
p. 375: Sheppard, Morris (Joe Vann) (photo at OHS)
p. 397: Smith, R.C. (John Ross to Tibbet to Smith)
p. 408: Starr, Milton (this interview is proven non-trustworthy)
p. 420: Thompson, Johnson (Joe Vann to Lowery to Thompson)
p. 422: Thompson, Victoria Taylor (Taylors)
p. 435: Vann, Lucinda (Jim Vann)
p. 445: Ward, Rochelle Allred—actually Rachel Aldrich Ward (Joe Beck)
p. 464: White, Charlotte Johnson (Ben Johnson)
p. 492: Wilson, Sarah (Ben Johnson)

Cherokee slave narratives not found in the Bakers' book: William Lee Starr, Dennis Vann, Sam Vann, Agnes Walker and Eliza Sanders Whitmire, plus the interview of J.J. Cape, the white pioneer who knew the founders of Foreman. All can be found online.

INDEX

BIOGRAPHICAL STATEMENTS OF CONTRIBUTORS

DR. T.L. (THOMAS LEE) BALLENGER was born in 1882 in Arkansas and died in 1987 in Tahlequah (at the age of 104). He was a long-term history professor at Northeastern State University from its beginning days as a Normal School, training teachers. He authored several books and articles. The NSU archive is in the campus library's Ballenger Room.

ART T. BURTON recently lectured on African Americans on the Western Frontier at Purdue University's Black Culture Center and is currently professor of history at South Suburban College in Illinois. He is the author of *Black, Red and Deadly: Black and Indian Gunfighters of Indian Territory*.

KAREN COODY COOPER retired from the Smithsonian's National Museum of the American Indian and has written *Cherokee Wampum*, *Spirited Encounters* and *Oklahoma Cherokee Baskets*. She also creates contemporary wampum weavings.

MARK A. HARRISON spent the last few years of his grandfather's life getting to know him. The stories he heard led Mark to a treasure-trove of history surrounding his family and their way of life among the Cherokee Indians. Today, Mark enjoys family research and visits to Oklahoma to see kinfolk and friends.

DAN HORSECHIEF has created fine art for more than twenty years working with oils and life-size bronze sculptures. He studied at the Institute of American Indian Arts in Santa Fe and was invited to show his art at Versailles, France. Having won multiple awards in area art shows, his most recent bronze monument honors Cherokee veterans.

Daniel F. Littlefield Jr. is director of the Sequoyah National Research Center at the University of Arkansas–Little Rock. He is the author of four books and a number of articles about the slaves and Freedmen of the so-called Five Civilized Tribes.

Tiya Miles is professor of history and Native American studies at the University of Michigan and author of two books about Afro-Cherokee history: *Ties that Bind* and *The House on Diamond Hill*. In 2011, she was a winner of the MacArthur Foundation's Genius Grant Award.

Celia E. Naylor is associate professor of history and African studies at Barnard College of Columbia University. In 2008, she authored *African Cherokees in Indian Territory: From Chattel to Citizens*.

Shirley Pettengill served as site manager of the Murrell Home for almost fifteen years. The 1845 Park Hill plantation home is operated by the Oklahoma Historical Society, focusing on the 1830s through the Civil War and up to the allotment period in the Cherokee Nation.

Reverend Joe Wilson is the president of Cherokees for Black Indian History Preservation Foundation and is retired from Eastar Health Systems. He grew up in the Lee Street neighborhood and is the assistant pastor of Historic First Baptist Church in Fort Gibson, Oklahoma.

Ty Wilson is a founder of Cherokees for Black Indian History Preservation Foundation. He is an entrepreneur and also works as a network technician for the Cherokee Nation. He grew up in the Lee Street neighborhood and produces an annual music and variety event, Green Country Roots Festival.

HOW THE BOOK CAME TO BE

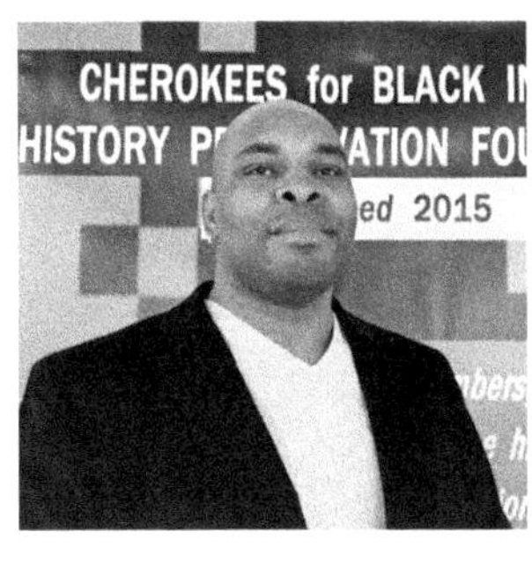

TY WILSON, founder of Cherokees for Black Indian History Preservation Foundation, and writer KAREN COODY COOPER decided to work together on *Oklahoma Black Cherokees* early in 2016. Wilson was raising money to create a cultural center in the abandoned Antioch Baptist Church (active when he was a youngster growing up in the neighborhood), and Cooper was looking for another history project when she discovered that the old church was just five blocks from where she lives. Tahlequah, Oklahoma, in the Cherokee Nation, is a history mecca with several rich archives, half a dozen museums and a crowd of reliable historians, all joining in revealing compelling stories of black Cherokee people.

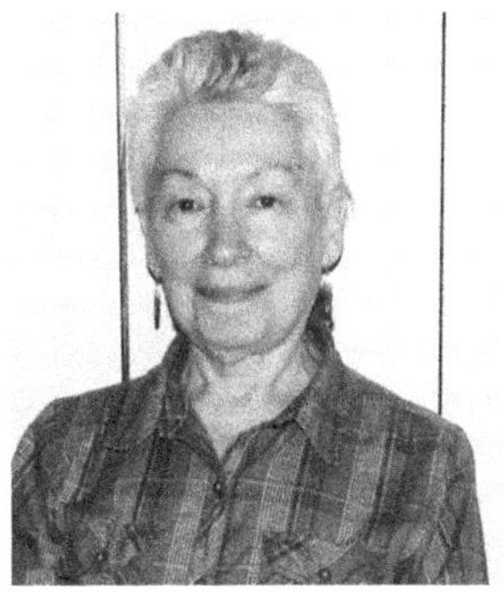

www.ingramcontent.com/pod-product-compliance
Lightning Source LLC
LaVergne TN
LVHW010938100826
845153LV00001B/78
9781540225726